SHARKS AND RAYS
OF HAWAI'I

SHARKS AND RAYS
OF HAWAI'I

BY
GERALD L. CROW
AND JENNIFER CRITES

PHOTOGRAPHY BY
JENNIFER CRITES

Mutual Publishing

Library of Congress Catalog Card Number: 2001097794

Design by Mardee Domingo Melton
Second Printing, July 2013

ISBN-10: 1-56647-498-1
ISBN-13: 978-1-56647-498-6

Mutual Publishing
1215 Center Street, Suite 210
Honolulu, Hawai'i 96816
Ph: (808) 732-1709
Fax: (808) 734-4094
e-mail: info@mutualpublishing.com
www.mutualpublishing.com

Printed in Korea.

Table of Contents

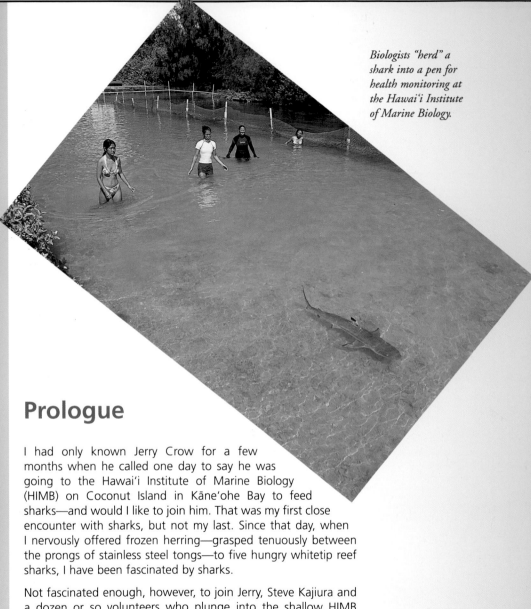

Biologists "herd" a shark into a pen for health monitoring at the Hawai'i Institute of Marine Biology.

Prologue

I had only known Jerry Crow for a few months when he called one day to say he was going to the Hawai'i Institute of Marine Biology (HIMB) on Coconut Island in Kāne'ohe Bay to feed sharks—and would I like to join him. That was my first close encounter with sharks, but not my last. Since that day, when I nervously offered frozen herring—grasped tenuously between the prongs of stainless steel tongs—to five hungry whitetip reef sharks, I have been fascinated by sharks.

Not fascinated enough, however, to join Jerry, Steve Kajiura and a dozen or so volunteers who plunge into the shallow HIMB ponds to herd the sharks into a smaller pen and then into a stretcher for measuring and health checks—I'll stay on dry land, thank you, and photograph the proceedings. But certainly fascinated enough to spend a week on Midway Atoll studying sharks in the class that Jerry teaches there each summer. And yes, I couldn't resist easing into Midway's crystal-clear water a couple of times to look for sharks.

Ancient Hawaiian weapons lined with sharks' teeth.

And fascinated enough to spend the past three years writing and photographing this book with Jerry. It's been an engaging adventure since we decided, one rainy day while on R&R in Hilo, that this book needed to be written. Since then, my journey into the realm of sharks and rays has been one of discovery.

I've absorbed an encyclopedia of information about Hawai'i's sharks and rays: how their gills gather oxygen from seawater, why a shark's electrosensory system urges it to bite boats, and the fact that young sharks "hatch" from eggs, among other intriguing facts.

I've met and worked with an oceanful of delightful and talented people—like artist Ruth Cabanting, whose eye-catching images of rays cavorting in Kāne'ohe Bay and a ceremonial cleansing at a shark heiau on the Big Island give me chicken skin. Then there's creative-art student Mike Salavea of Farrington High School, who produced our illustrations detailing the male and female shark reproductive systems; and Elaine Cheung, who studies art at the University of Hawai'i and who composed the shark gills drawing.

Also a U.H. art student, Audra Furuichi's multidimensional talent includes not only the beautiful technical illustrations, Hawai'i's Ocean Habitats and The Shark Eye, which she crafted for this book, but also remarkable freehand sketches of people, whom she captures with flourishing pencil strokes while riding the bus. The color-rich and compelling paintings of 13-year-old Jonah Okano, an art student at 'Iolani, vividly portray the relationships between ancient Hawaiians and sharks. Jonah is talented and a winner of many art awards; he's friendly, diligent and responsible when it comes to honoring his commitments—a pleasure to work with, as were all of our artists.

There were struggles to be sure. Finding a balance between accurate scientific terminology and language more understandable to the rest of us nonscientists was a constant challenge. As Jerry and I worked, the book expanded like multiplying tilapia in a fishpond. Everything was interesting—we didn't want to leave out any of the good stuff. So here it is, finally! In your hands you hold a three-year odyssey. And the best we, as authors, can hope for is that you enjoy reading it as much as we enjoyed putting it together. Savor the journey.

Aloha—Jennifer Crites

Acknowledgments

This book would not have been possible without the dedication, determination and hard work of shark and ray researchers around the world whose efforts have dramatically increased our knowledge about these remarkable animals. The authors are particularly saddened by the loss of Don Nelson and Perry Gilbert, whose infectious personalities, zest for life and willingness to share knowledge and experiences will be sorely missed. Also missed is the University of Hawai'i's Albert Tester. His vast contributions to the body of knowledge about Hawaiian shark sensory systems, feeding behavior and biology made this book a reality.

Many people volunteered their valuable time and resources to make *Sharks and Rays of Hawai'i* what we hope will be a definitive reference work and popular standard. The list of contributing photographers alone reads like a Who's Who of the ocean-research community: Jack Randall; Leonard Compagno; George Balazs; Brad Wetherbee; Gordon Hubbell; Greg Cailliet; Bob Humphreys; the Oceanic Society's Cynthia Vanderlip; Ian "Shark" Gordon of Animal Planet fame; John Henderson, John Naughton, John Buchanan, Chad Yoshinaga, Andrew Vatter and Joe Arceneaux of National Marine Fisheries Service (NMFS); Brian Midson at Hawai'i Undersea Research Laboratory; Larry Ellis; Steve Kajiura; Betsey Rasmussen; Susan Rickards; and the Waikīkī Aquarium. Others sharing their photos with our readers include Mike Connolly; Eric Le Feuvre; Roger Pfeffer; Thomas Fenske; Ray Boland; Steve Huffman; Kendra Choquette; Michael Pollack; Young Brothers; longtime free-diver and local boy Lymon Higa; Farrington High School science teacher Pat Kesling-Wood; and Big Island dive master Keller Laros, who contributed pictures of Lefty the manta ray. To all of you, our sincere thanks for your generosity.

Many thanks also to Sandra Raredon and Susan Jewett of the Smithsonian Institution, National Museum of Natural History, Division of Fishes, for taking digital pictures, at our request, of the spongehead catshark and Hawaiian lantern shark—both rare type specimens collected from Hawaiian waters in 1904 and 1902, respectively—and the diamond stingray; to Steve Kajiura for lending us his hammerhead and other shark and ray jaws as subjects for our camera; to Mike Connolly for his extensive computer help; to Bob Humphreys at NMFS for providing access to his frozen shark collection; to John Hoover and Bruce Mundy for their advice and support; to Mike Laurs and Edith Chave for their continued assistance; to Caroline Julian for arranging our photo shoot at Sea Life Park; and to staff members at Sea Life Park and the Waikīkī Aquarium for their help in making those photo sessions successful. To Arnold Suzumoto of Bishop Museum's

The dorsal fin of a blacktip reef shark ripples the water's surface in an atrium at the Mauna Lani Resort on the Big Island.

Ichthyology collection we extend our grateful appreciation for allowing us to photograph the valuable research collection under his care and for giving freely of his time and expertise over several Fridays to help us accomplish our task.

We also owe a debt of gratitude to our chapter reviewers who diligently scanned every fact and made sure all information was technically accurate: Brad Wetherbee; Bob Hueter; Steve Kajiura; Chris Lowe; Carl Luer; Tim Tricas; Tom Webster; Russell Ito; John Wourms; Bruce Carlson and Cindy Hunter of the Waikīkī Aquarium; Craig Thomas; Susan Scott (and the other members of Jennifer's writers' group: Kristin McAndrews, Kaethe Kauffman and Michaelyn Chou for their valuable wordsmithing advice); Leslie Hayashi, Cie McMullin, Leonard McMullin, Evan McMullin and Annie Green for their comments and support; and Herb Kawainui Kane for his review of our Hawaiians and Sharks chapter.

Leonard Compagno deserves special recognition for his dedication to the process of identifying sharks and for the volumes of information he has compiled, paving the way for other researchers and making it possible for the authors to identify and describe the 40 shark species present in Hawaiian waters.

Our thanks also to Chuck Johnston, publisher of *Hawaii Fishing News,* for sharing his readers' shark and ray stories with us and for printing our request for more stories in two editions. Glenn Takenaka, Andrew Vatter, Dale Sarver, Kendra Choquette and Richard Pyle were all kind enough to contribute tales of their encounters.

We are deeply indebted to all of you and to the many others not specifically mentioned here who have helped to make this book a useful addition to Hawai'i's marine literature.

from Gerald L. Crow

There is not enough space here to list all the people who have had an impact on my career as a biologist and who have, in many ways, supported my interest in sharks and rays. In particular, though, I'd like to extend my thanks to Raymond Keyes and Frank Murru for teaching me how to appreciate and care for sharks, and to Carl Luer and Betsey Rasmussen for their support, encouragement and good company while I was still a young, untried researcher; to Sonny Gruber and Steve Kaiser for giving me valuable experiences with free-living sharks in the field; to Jack Randall for sharing his experience and support whenever it was needed; to my research partners Brad Wetherbee and Chris Lowe for helping me bring to light the forgotten data from shark-control and Northwestern Hawaiian Islands fisheries programs, and the University of Hawai'i's Zoology Department for maintaining that data and allowing us unfettered access to it; to Gordon Grau and Kim Holland for research access to the Hawai'i Institute of Marine Biology's shark pens; and certainly to Bruce Carlson and the entire staff at the Waikīkī Aquarium for their assistance, support and putting up with my shark-related requests for fourteen years.

Sharks are everywhere in Hawai'i—even on the corner of Queen and South Streets.

The ancestors of today's sharks lived 450 million years ago.

Ian Gordon

Introduction

Forty species of sharks and nine species of rays live in the ocean surrounding the Hawaiian Islands and yet we know so little about them—a consequence, perhaps, of the ubiquitous marine environment concealing more than it reveals. It's as if the sea has posted a cautionary sign: Glimpses Only!

For the most part, sharks and rays don't get much respect. Rays are largely ignored except by recreational divers who seek them out as photographic subjects. When sharks are noticed at all, it's as nuisances or imminent danger—for taking a bite out of a surfboard (or a surfer), for stealing and damaging fishing gear, and for eating prized 'ahi (tuna) struggling on longline hooks. Sharks themselves are rarely eaten in Hawai'i and were usually caught accidentally during tuna-fishing operations. Only since the early 1990s, when prices for fins increased dramatically, have sharks garnered a different kind of attention—as a source of the prime ingredient for shark-fin soup.

Still, there are those who find sharks and rays interesting, even intriguing, and who want to get beyond the shark-as-terrorizing-monster image to learn more about these mysterious animals. It is for you that this book has been written. In the following pages we've included a shark's-eye view of Hawai'i's volcanic origins, from ancient Colahan Seamount in the Northwestern Hawaiian Islands to the newest island, Lo'ihi, growing over the pressure-cooker hot spot just south of the Big Island. You'll also find up-to-date fact sheets on the sharks and rays that inhabit the nearshore and deep-water ocean realm around the Hawaiian Islands; a chapter discussing the early Hawaiians' relationships with sharks; stories from people who've experienced close encounters of the shark or ray kind; insightful illustrations by Hawai'i's art students; and photographs of unusual sharks and rays. In fact, this book contains hundreds of never-before-published photographs of such rare species as the crocodile shark, false cat shark, and frilled shark, among others.

We hope that each chapter invites you, our readers, to explore and understand the fascinating world of sharks and rays, and thereby discover a new awareness of the role these animals play in maintaining the ocean's delicate balance of life.

CHAPTER 1

HAWAI'I'S OCEANIC ORIGINS: THE UNDERSEA WORLD

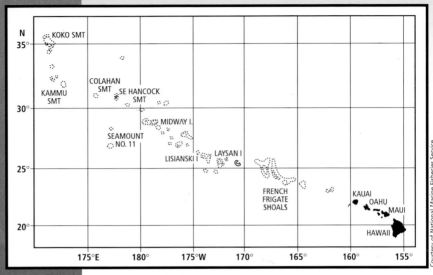

Courtesy of National Marine Fisheries Service.

Hawaiian Islands

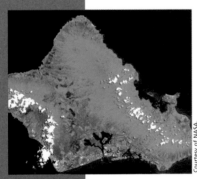

Courtesy of NASA.

A satellite view of O'ahu.

Hawai'i's sharks and rays congregate around some of the most isolated islands in the world—almost in the center of the Pacific Ocean. Geographic maps place Hawai'i's capital, Honolulu, 2,400 miles from the west coast of North America and 3,800 miles from Japan. Anchorage, Alaska sits 2,800 miles to the north, with Canberra, Australia, 5,200 miles to the south—and almost no land in between.

This secluded group of islands known as the Hawaiian archipelago stretches across 1,600 miles of ocean and consists of 132 islands, islets, sandcays, and reefs. Hawai'i's eight main "high" islands—all inhabited except for Kaho'olawe—make up 99% of the total land area. With the notable exception of Midway Atoll, the remainder of the island chain—the Northwestern Hawaiian Islands—includes mostly uninhabited rocks and atolls (known as "low" islands), as well as reefs, banks and submerged seamounts.

The West Maui mountains and Kaua'i's Kalalau Valley show off their volcanic, high-island terrain.

Still over the hot spot, the Big Island of Hawai'i oozes red-hot lava, adding to its volcanic land mass.

Five-million years old, Kaua'i is still a high island, but weathering has begun.

The Hawaiian Islands originated as undersea volcanoes, as opposed to continental islands, which are chunks of land that have broken free of a continental mass. Volcanic islands erupt from the sea floor as bubbling, churning, spitting lava that solidifies, eventually breaking the ocean's surface and forming mountains such as the Big Island's Mauna Kea, which soars 13,796 feet above sea level. Each of Hawai'i's volcanic islands was born over a hot spot—a magma plume jetting from the earth's mantle—at roughly 19° north and 155° west latitude. Each island is also anchored to the Pacific tectonic plate, the largest of five shifting slabs of rock making up the earth's crust in the Pacific. As this plate moves northwest at 3.5 inches a year, the established islands travel with it, while new islands such as Lo'ihi emerge over the hot spot at the archipelago's southeasterly end.

You could say that the hot spot and the Pacific Plate act like a slow-moving assembly line, creating new islands and moving them along in a northwesterly direction. Colahan Seamount, once a high island and now just a flat-topped underwater mountain near the far northwest end of the chain, is 39 million years old,

The forces of erosion are evident on Kaua'i's
Nā Pali coast.

Coral reefs fringe Waikīkī's shoreline and could
someday cover the island of O'ahu.

George Balazs

Midway Atoll, once a high island, is now
sinking into the sea.

predating the emergence of Hawai'i's coral reefs
34 million years ago. Further down the line,
Midway Atoll claims 28 million years of existence.
Kaua'i weighs in at 5 million; O'ahu, 3.5 million;
and the Big Island of Hawai'i, less than one
million. When an island migrates away from the
hot spot it no longer grows and begins a process
of breakdown. Eroded by the action of waves,
rainfall, lichens, and wind, and pushed downward by its own weight, the mountainous island
eventually sinks into the ocean and becomes a
seamount, a high spot on the ocean floor.

Approximately 1,200 miles from O'ahu, Midway
Atoll in the Northwestern Hawaiian Islands illus-
trates an intermediate step in the creation and
breakdown of a volcanic island. Now a National
Wildlife Refuge and home to 150 people who
work there, Midway's three low islands jut out
from the ocean's surface no more than twelve
feet at their highest point. Actually, Midway's
basalt—its volcanic base—rests more than 500
feet below sea level, the result of erosion. Visitors
to the atoll may find it hard to believe that they
are standing on more than 500 feet of coral that
originally surrounded the island as a reef and
then covered it as the basalt settled into the
ocean. Over time, these coral remnants left
behind by reef-building animals continue to
break down, and someday, Midway, like Colahan
Seamount, will slip below the waves. Such
seamounts alter ocean currents and can become
productive areas of ocean-life diversity, lucrative
locations for fishing fleets, and a favored hang-
out for sharks.

The ancestors of today's sharks ruled the oceans some 450 million years ago—well before the creation of the Hawaiian Islands, but in a relatively recent period of earth's 4,500-million-year history. These boneless shark primogenitors left us a record of their existence in fossils that consist primarily of teeth, fin spines and dermal denticles (scales). Biologists believe that stingrays evolved roughly 60 million years ago, and the modern sharks we recognize today own a fossil record reaching back 100 million years. The oldest record of a great white shark tells us that this predator existed 60 to 65 million years ago, while its now-extinct relative, the gigantic, megatoothed megalodon (*Carcharodon megalodon*), cruised the oceans 10 to 25 million years ago.

Fossilized great white shark teeth (not from Hawai'i).

Sharks and rays fall into the group called cartilaginous fishes because instead of bone, their skeletons are made of cartilage. Worldwide, this group includes some 1,000 species, including 376 sharks and 494 rays. Since new species are discovered on a semi-regular basis—the first megamouth shark was captured in Hawaiian waters as recently as 1976—researchers believe that still more will be found and added to the list.

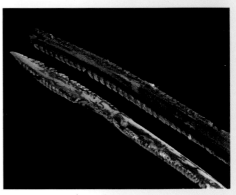

Stingray spines are among the few clues left by prehistoric sharks and rays.

Sharks and rays inhabit all parts of the ocean around Hawai'i, both coastal areas and the three open-ocean regions: near-surface (epipelagic), mid-water (mesopelagic), and deep-ocean (bathypelagic)—between and around islands. Newly born blacktip reef sharks, still unsure of their surroundings, occasionally wash up along the shoreline and wriggle back into the waves at bustling Waikīkī Beach, and deep-water bluntnose sixgill sharks and sixgill stingrays appear in the spotlights of submersibles at depths of 4,725 and 3,117 feet, respectively. Although stingrays usually forage for food at or near the ocean bottom, one species—the pelagic stingray—often feeds at depths of 246 to 338 feet in areas where the ocean floor lies thousands of feet below.

A shortspine spurdog shark cruises past the window of a Hawai'i Undersea Research Laboratory (HURL) deep-sea submersible.

Both sharks and rays usually occupy preferred habitats that serve as their home ranges, and the locations of these home ranges can vary with the species and age of the animal. The adult scalloped hammerhead, for example, swims into bays and other protected areas to give birth and then returns to deeper waters offshore. A blacktip reef shark spends its entire life along the coastal shoreline in and near coral reefs, while an oceanic whitetip shark never comes close to shore, preferring to hunt and pup in the formless environs of the open ocean. Hawai'i's blue sharks are highly nomadic and travel throughout the North Pacific Ocean. Shark

Courtesy of HURL.

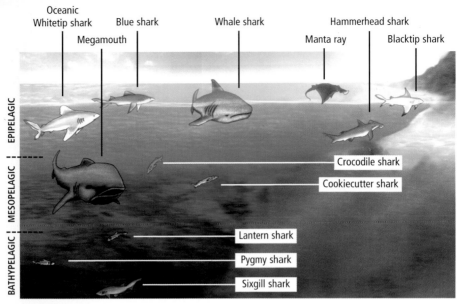

EPIPELAGIC

MESOPELAGIC

BATHYPELAGIC

Oceanic Whitetip shark

Megamouth

Blue shark

Whale shark

Manta ray

Hammerhead shark

Blacktip shark

Crocodile shark

Cookiecutter shark

Lantern shark

Pygmy shark

Sixgill shark

Hawai'i's Ocean Habitats. Illustration by Audra Furuichi.

Hammerhead pups search for food in Kāne'ohe Bay.

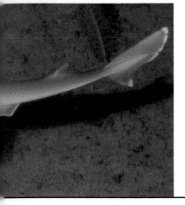

researchers speculate that great white sharks visit Hawai'i seasonally, possibly following the humpback whale calving migrations. And the parasitic cookiecutter shark appears to swim from the surface to great depths, following the daily migration of zooplankton.

Physical environmental factors also affect habitat selection, and many sharks and rays use coral reefs, drop-offs, slopes and submarine canyons as reference points within their home ranges. Currents, the presence or absence of light, pressure, water temperature and oxygen concentrations can also influence where an animal decides to live. The Galapagos shark, numerous around Midway and other Northwestern Hawaiian Islands, frequently chooses areas where strong currents surge past points of land and converging currents push water away from shore. The gray reef shark prefers the leeward sides of islands as well as clear water with rugged sea-floor terrain and strong currents. And sharks such as the bluntnose sixgill opt for inky-dark, deep-water habitats.

Even liver enzymes play a role in habitat selection. Enzymes that work effectively at pressures below 1,600 feet do not work above this depth, causing some body processes to malfunction when a shark or ray leaves its normal depth range.

Jack Randall

Probably the most important factor determining habitat distribution is temperature. Around Hawai'i, coastal sharks and rays have adapted to a water temperature of 68-79°F, whereas deep-water species prefer a colder 40-54°F. Although seawater appears to cool gradually from the sunlit surface to the deepest trenches, appearances can be deceiving. The thermocline, an unstable, constantly shifting water mass characterized by rapid temperature change, generally occurs somewhere between the 325- and 1,000-foot level in the Pacific and separates coastal and epipelagic from deep-water sharks and rays. However, some open-ocean, epipelagic sharks such as the shortfin mako come equipped with an internal heating system that allows them to penetrate the thermocline and swim into the colder waters below it for short periods of time, presumably to search for food.

Above: Sharks choose their home ranges with specific features in mind. A gray reef shark prefers strong currents and rugged sea-floor terrain.

Right: Some sharks and rays need more oxygen than others. This spotted eagle ray cruises in a shallow, oxygen-rich lagoon.

A long-distance traveler, the whale shark can migrate over thousands of miles in the formless ocean depths.

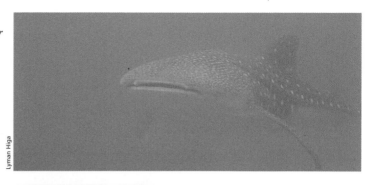

Lyman Higa

Jack Randall

A whitetip reef shark eyes a potential meal.

Temperature also influences the amount of oxygen in the water, and to survive, sharks and rays must absorb oxygen through their gills, with some animals requiring more oxygen than others. Biologists previously considered concentrations of 2 to 4 parts oxygen per million parts water as the minimum levels for survival; but recently in California's Santa Barbara Basin, they found that a prickly shark swimming at a depth of 1,122 feet in 44°F water needed an oxygen concentration of less than one (0.56) part per million. With startling new finds such as this one, it's clear we still have a great deal to learn about sharks and rays.

Since Hawai'i is so remote and its origins volcanic, how did sharks and rays get here? Long-distance travelers such as blue, oceanic whitetip and whale sharks could have followed currents or just arrived in the normal course of their wanderings. Blacktip and scalloped hammerhead—coastal sharks normally associated with land masses—are also semi-oceanic, and this fact might have allowed them to reach Hawai'i by island-hopping. Pacific seamounts—at least 30,000 of them rising from the ocean floor to a height roughly four times that of Diamond Head—could have acted as stepping stones for deep-sea sharks in their journeys to Hawai'i. However, coastal-hugging whitetip reef sharks tend to be sluggish swimmers who spend a lot of time resting in caves. How they arrived in Hawai'i remains just one of the many ongoing and intriguing mysteries of the sea.

CHAPTER 2

ANATOMY

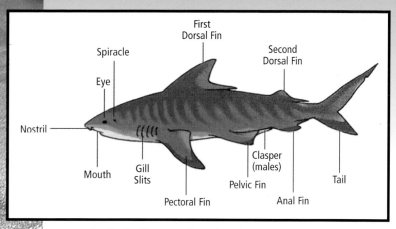

Parts of a Shark. Illustration by Mike Salavea.

Although sharks and rays are fish, they are different in many ways from tuna, mackerel, salmon and others in the category we know as bony fish. Sharks and rays do not have bones. Instead, their skeletons are made of cartilage. They have five to seven external gill openings, no swim bladder for buoyancy, paired pectoral and pelvic fins, and an upper jaw that is not firmly attached to the brain casing.

Most bony fish, on the other hand, have a swim bladder to keep them afloat, a single external gill opening (covered by an operculum), and a variety of different fin configurations. During reproduction, bony fish usually expel eggs and sperm into the surrounding water, whereas sharks rely on internal fertilization—males transfer sperm directly to the female via appendages known as claspers.

Unlike cartilaginous sharks and rays, this bluestripe snapper has a skeleton made of bone.

9

Courtesy of Waikiki Aquarium.

Skin spots will turn into stripes as this tiger shark matures.

Andrew Vatter, NMFS-PIAO

Sharks come in a wide variety of shapes and sizes, from the massive 45-foot whale shark to the tiny six-inch pygmy shark. Their bodies might be tan, brown, gray or black; or they might be marked with stripes or spots. Five to seven visible gill slits are located on each side of the body. Some sharks, such as the angel and wobbegong, are flat and are sometimes mistaken for rays. Others, such as the mako, have torpedo-shaped bodies, or are bulky, like the whale shark. Even their eyes can be different colors—black, brown or green.

Fins, too, show variations. A shark might have one or two dorsal fins, some with pointed spines (for protection); and an anal fin can be present or absent. Some sharks, especially slow-moving bottom dwellers, have a large spiracle—an opening that sucks water in and over the gills—behind each eye. In powerful, fast-swimming sharks, water reaches the gills through the mouth, and the spiracles are either small or nonexistent.

Teeth can be triangular (great white), one-piece saw-blade (cookiecutter), fang-like (crocodile shark) or any of a multitude of shapes and sizes; and because the upper jaw moves away from the brain case during feeding, a shark can thrust this mobile jaw almost out of its mouth to encircle larger prey than it could otherwise tackle. Scales, too, vary in size and shape depending on the species. In other words, sharks are a diverse group and no one description fits them all.

Rays are more homogeneous. They all have a flattened body shape, although some, such as the torpedo ray, are equipped with a swimming tail, and others, a narrow whip-like tail that may or may not sport a sharp protective spine. As a result of this flattening of the body, sense organs such as the lateral line and ampullae of Lorenzini (see **Chapter 3: Senses**) cover a large area over

Can you name these sharks? Slightly different dorsal fins help identify look-alike sharks. From front to back: sandbar, blacktip and Galapagos.

Courtesy of HURL.

Round-bodied torpedo rays stun their victims with an electric shock.

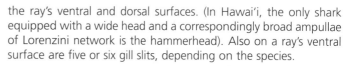

Top: A velvet dogfish scale showing peaks and valleys.

Center: Star-shaped manta ray head scales.

Bottom: False cat shark scales look like tiny globules (preserved, BPBM).

Brad Wetherbee

the ray's ventral and dorsal surfaces. (In Hawai'i, the only shark equipped with a wide head and a correspondingly broad ampullae of Lorenzini network is the hammerhead). Also on a ray's ventral surface are five or six gill slits, depending on the species.

Instead of shark-like pectoral fins, rays have modified pectoral fins called wings. These muscular wings are especially well developed in the eagle and manta rays and are supported by a cartilaginous skeleton more extensive than the pectoral skeleton in sharks. A ray's mouth is on the underside of its body and, like sharks, the jaw is loosely attached to the skull so that it can be thrust downward for suction feeding on the ocean bottom or grasping prey directly below the mouth. Some specializations occurring in rays include muscles that produce an electric shock (torpedo ray), cephalic horns that help in the capture of food (manta ray), and the venom glands of stingrays.

Scales

Called placoid scales or dermal denticles because of their similarity to shark teeth, scales surround the body of the shark. Not so with rays, which have a greatly reduced number of scales—possibly because they habitually bury themselves in sand and may need smoother bodies and less resistance for this process. But rays have skin protection in the form of body mucus.

Scales are thought to provide protection from predators and from abrasion, reduce frictional drag, and shield bioluminescent and sensory organs on the skin. Scales of active swimming sharks are designed with sharp peaks and small valleys running from front to back so that water moving from the shark's head to its tail will flow over them efficiently. The mako and silky sharks' scales have a smaller basal plate (anchoring area), which allows water to pass more quickly around the scale. But the prickly shark, a slow-moving bottom dweller, has large thorn-like scales projecting out from its body.

Some sharks have scales that are thinner and equipped with cross ridges and pits (similar to a golf ball) to increase hydrodynamic efficiency. In fact, the outer hulls of many U.S. Navy submarines have, in recent years, been covered with a layer of pitted rubber skin—much like shark scales—in an effort to reduce drag and noise, making the sub harder to detect. Also, as reported in the journal *Nature* (Aug. 5, 1999), a transparent and ribbed plastic film modeled on shark scales is now being attached to the outside of some jet airliners to reduce drag by up to 8 percent (representing a fuel savings of about 1.5 percent).

In some sharks, scales grow inside the mouth, an adaptation that may aid in holding or breaking up food before swallowing. The horn shark's scales are sharper on the leading edges of its pectoral fins, giving the newly hatching shark an edge while breaking out of its egg case. Old scales, once they are no longer useful, turn white, self-destruct and are replaced.

Fin spines, present on the shortspine spurdog and a few other sharks, are larger yet similar in structure to scales, but lack the outer enamel layer.

Above: A sharp, pointed spine in front of the dorsal fin serves as protection for this shortspine spurdog shark.

Below: Skin pores on the head of this sand tiger shark lead to the electrosensory ampullae of Lorenzini (preserved BPBM).

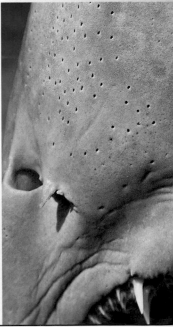

Skin

Shark skin varies in thickness, depending on the species and sex of the animal. The skin of female blue sharks, for example, is at least twice as thick as that of the males—possibly because, during copulation, males severely bite and slash the skin of their mates and the thicker skin helps prevent serious damage.

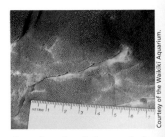

Courtesy of the Waikīkī Aquarium.

Jagged mating slashes mark the skin of a female tiger shark.

The outer layer of skin, or epidermis, contains mucus cells, bioluminescent photophores in some species, and the openings for the lateral line canal pores and ampullae of Lorenzini. Beneath the epidermis is the dermis, the growth and attachment area for scales. The dermis also houses the electrical receptors of the ampullae of Lorenzini and the canals that make up the lateral line system.

A shark's skin can actually help the shark swim faster. As swimming speed increases from slow to fast, the shark's internal body pressure increases tenfold. As a result of this pressure, the skin becomes stiffer, acting like an external tendon on the adjoining muscles and transmitting muscular force to the tail.

Below: The teeth of a juvenile great white shark (bottom of photo) are narrower than those of an adult great white. Upper jaw.

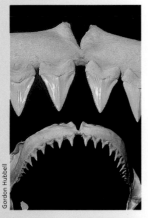

Gordon Hubbell

In the dermis, near the border of the epidermis, dark-pigmented cells called melanophores can change a shark's color. If strong light rays enter the eye or the light-sensitive pineal organ on top of the head, they can stimulate the pituitary gland to release a melanophore-stimulating hormone into the bloodstream. This hormone is absorbed by the melanophores, causing them to expand and spread out, thus darkening the skin. Research with scalloped hammerhead sharks in a shallow pond at the Hawai'i Institute of Marine Biology has shown that a shark's skin darkens when exposed to bright light. Both sharks and rays appear to be able to darken or lighten their skin color to match their surroundings. Skin darkening can also help protect these animals from the harmful effects of ultraviolet light.

Above: Rows of tiger shark teeth migrate into feeding position at the front edge of the jaw.

Teeth and Jaws

Shark teeth typically grow in rows, and as individual teeth fall out, they are replaced by new teeth. Teeth are anchored in connective tissue covering the jaw cartilage (a stiff base that acts like bone). As teeth mature and are pulled forward, the anchoring tissue also migrates forward. Not all sharks, however, shed their teeth one at a time. The cookiecutter, for example, sheds its entire tooth plate at once. Tooth replacement might take eight to ten days per row or up to five weeks per row. The rate appears to be temperature-sensitive, with cold-water sharks having the slowest replacement rate. Nurse sharks studied had a summer shedding rate of 9 to 21 days per row, while the winter rate was 51 to 70 days per row.

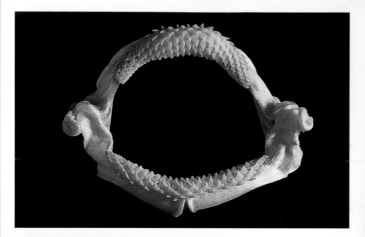

Left: The male pelagic stingray uses its sharp teeth for holding onto food and its mate.

Below: An eagle ray's pavement-shaped upper and lower teeth plates.

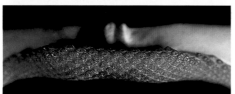

Left: Brown stingray teeth are adapted for crushing shells.

A shark's teeth appear to increase in size with increasing body length. In some species like the great white, tooth shape can change as diet changes during different life stages, becoming wider and more triangular in older sharks. Also, the replacement rate might slow down once the shark reaches maturity.

Teeth begin their development in the dental lamina, a fold of skin on the jaw cartilage. They start as buds and grow through successive stages of mineralization until they are functional. Both the enamel and dentine layers increase in thickness as the tooth moves forward. Even when the enamel has stopped growing, determining the size of the tooth, the dentine continues to expand at the expense of the pulp cavity. Teeth grow to their full size before reaching the margin of the jaw, so that several rows may be fully developed and waiting in the wings, so to speak, before they are actually used in feeding.

Shaped for cruising, the long pectoral fins of an oceanic whitetip shark could be a blueprint for aircraft wings.

In contrast to the sharply pointed teeth of most sharks, rays in general have flat, crushing teeth for breaking up crustacean and clam shells. Some rays, such as the male pelagic stingray, however, have sharp, triangular teeth adapted for grabbing and holding a mate during courtship. Teeth are shed one by one as they wear out, although the males of some stingray species may shed their sharp reproductive teeth seasonally. Eagle rays' teeth don't look like teeth at all and are often referred to as pavement- or cobblestone-shaped plates.

Fins and Locomotion
Pectoral Fins and Lift

In fast-swimming sharks, paired pectoral fins act like hydrofoils or airplane wings—flat on the bottom, thicker and rounded along the front surface, thinner toward the back, and angled slightly downward in the direction of the tail—to produce hydrodynamic lift. The flat underside of the head also helps create lift, and the torpedo-like body is ideally shaped for efficient cruising.

Above: A scalloped hammerhead's wide head provides additional lift to compensate for its short pectoral fins.

In the scalloped hammerhead, which has smaller pectoral fins than other sharks of its size, the expanded head (cephalofoil) compensates by providing additional lift. Blue sharks and oceanic whitetips, on the other hand, have long pectoral fins for gliding in oceanic currents. Some of the deep-water pelagic sharks have very small pectoral fins, yet are almost neutrally buoyant due to a large amount of liver oil (a sort of built-in flotation device).

However, pectoral fins have other uses besides lift. They can be angled downward for a rapid turn, steep descent, or other change in direction. They may also be used as posturing displays or social signals, perhaps having a role in dominance behavior between sharks.

James D. Watt/Innerspace Visions

A bigeye thresher shark's grooved pectoral and pelvic fins.

Like birds, spotted eagle rays flap their wings.

Most rays, on the other hand, maneuver through the water using modified pectoral fins called wings (guitarfish and sawfish rays can use their tails for propulsion). Eagle and manta rays with triangular bodies flap their wings, gliding through water the way many birds fly through air. Round-shaped stingrays do not fly in the same manner. Their wings generate a wave or ripple that moves along the edges of the wings from front to back, increasing in height and pushing the surrounding water aside to generate thrust.

Tails

A shark's tail is heterocercal, meaning the upper lobe is longer than the lower lobe. The backbone, which extends into the upper lobe, helps strengthen the tail, giving the shark support for extra forward thrust. In the past, it was thought that this thrust had a downward projectory, which was counterbalanced by the pectoral fins. Recently, however, scientists have discovered that it actually gives the shark a slightly upward momentum.

Above: This visitor to Sea Life Park makes friends with a brown stingray.

Below: A section of backbone strengthens a shark's tail.

A quick look at the tail and an observer can easily tell whether the shark is a fast or slow swimmer. Firm, powerful tails provide a great deal of thrust. It's been roughly estimated that the muscular blue shark can swim 23.5 miles per hour (mph) to maintain its position against a current, while slowing down to an average of one mph at normal cruising speed. Another fast shark, the shortfin mako, has been credited with 40 mph during short bursts of speed, and a great white has been clocked at 20 mph in full attack mode and under two miles per hour while cruising. Some tails—like that of the pygmy shark—can be extremely small and not provide much thrust at all. Others are modified for practical reasons. The upper lobe of a thresher shark's tail, for example, is almost as long as its body. While circling a school of fish, the thresher whips its long tail back and forth, stunning some of its victims and forcing the rest into a tighter ball until it is ready to turn into the densely swimming mass and feed.

A bigeye thresher shark uses its whip-like tail to stun fish.

Top: A nearly symmetrical tail helps make a shark such as the mako a powerfully fast swimmer.

Above: Upper lobe noticeably longer than lower, the tail of a crocodile shark provides less thrust than a symmetrical tail.

Most rays found in Hawaiian waters have a rope-like tail. One exception is the torpedo ray, an electric ray with a paddle-like tail. Although its tail provides propulsion, the torpedo ray is a sluggish swimmer, relying on its electric-shock adaptation rather than speed to capture prey.

Pelvic Fins and Keel

keel ➡

Pelvic fins, although small, provide their share of lift. And a keel at the base of the tail of more powerful, fast-swimming sharks (mako and great whites, for example), creates a slight turbulence, diverting the fast flow of water along the shark's body and allowing the tail more freedom of movement. The keel might also reinforce the tail, strengthening it for fast swimming.

A brown stingray's rope-like tail is covered with large, prickly scales called tubercles.

A rounded keel adds thrust to the tail of a mako or great white shark.

Dorsal fins help sharks stay upright while swimming.

Dorsal Fins

Last, but not least, the dorsal fin helps stabilize the shark so that it swims straight and doesn't roll from side to side. The trailing edge of the first dorsal fin creates a vacuum that extends to the tail, making the tail's forward thrust slightly more efficient, and allowing the shark to conserve energy while swimming.

On some sharks, a mid-dorsal ridge (top shark) runs between the two dorsal fins (preserved, BPBM).

Muscles

Sharks swim by oscillating their bodies from side to side, while most rays use a pectoral up-and-down motion or a wave (described in **Pectoral Fins** above). But muscles are not just essential for swimming. They also provide the impetus for breathing, feeding, blood-pumping, clasper movements in mating, fin and eye movement and digestion.

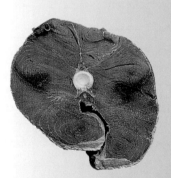

Sharks and rays have two major muscle masses: red and white. The red is typically located along the side of the body, and the more actively swimming sharks (mako and great white) have a greater proportion of red folded within white muscle. Red muscle allows an active shark to maintain its cruising speed indefinitely under normal conditions.

Some sharks' muscles house a network of blood vessels known as the rete mirable (dark areas).

White muscle makes up about 89% of the total muscle mass of the blue shark and is used primarily for fast sprint swimming. This type of muscle receives less oxygen than red, quickly becomes anaerobic, and cannot sustain speed for any length of time.

Some of Hawai'i's sharks—the shortfin mako, great white and pelagic thresher—have unique nets of blood vessels present in lateral body muscles, eyes and brain. In this rete mirable, as each net is called, blood picks up heat from working muscles, traps it, and returns it to the muscles, creating a sectional heating system within the shark. These remarkable systems raise the temperature as much as 9-18°F above that of the surrounding water. The eye and brain retes are thought to buffer the effects of a rapid temperature drop as the shark dives into deeper waters.

Sharks tagged with electronic transmitters have provided corroboration of this process: A great white swimming in 64°F water had a stomach temperature of 77°F (the stomach is near the red-muscle rete), and a mako in 69.8°F water registered a deep lateral muscle temperature of 80.6°F. On an interesting note, retes do not warm up the cold-blooded shark's heart. The transmitters indicated that heart temperatures for both sharks were equal to the surrounding water temperature.

Recently, researchers have discovered that manta rays and devil rays have retes around their brains.

The skeletal chondrocranium and jaws of a hammerhead shark are made of cartilage.

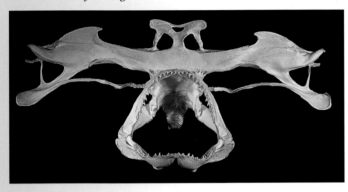

Skeleton

Skeletons of both sharks and rays are made of cartilage that is strengthened by calcification. In deep-water and some oceanic sharks, this calcification is reduced, making the shark lighter in weight and thus helping to increase buoyancy.

The brain case, or chondrocranium, protects the brain, nasal organs, eyes and inner ears. Attached to this brain case is a vertebral column made up of individual sections of backbone called centra, which vary in number from 60 to 477, depending on the species. Extending from these centra are small ribs that can be absent in some sharks and rays. A large surface area on both jaws supports strong biting muscles, and the shark's upper jaw is not firmly attached to the chondrocranium, giving it flexibility during biting.

Skeletal extensions inside the male claspers become longer and calcify with the onset of sexual maturity.

Ringed centra along the length of a shark's backbone.

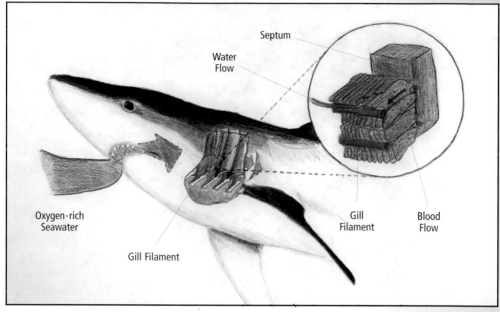

Gills. Illustration by Elaine Cheung.

Like human lungs, a shark's red gill filaments exchange oxygen and carbon dioxide.

A manta ray's gills (above pencil) (preserved, BPBM).

A spiracle behind the eye of this shortspine spurdog shark allows water to enter the body and pass over the gills.

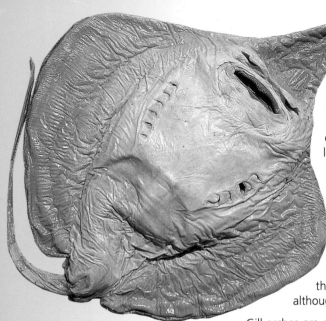

Gills

Gills allow a shark to take in oxygen by exchanging respiratory gasses (oxygen and carbon dioxide) between the shark and its aquatic environment. In bottom-dwelling sharks and rays, paired openings called spiracles—each one located between the eye and gill slits—help to pull water into the body where it passes over the gills and out through the gill slits. In more active, rapidly swimming sharks—which must sustain a critical swimming speed in order to supply enough oxygen to the body—the main flow of water to the gills is through the mouth, although small spiracles may be present.

A sixgill stingray (preserved, BPBM).

Gill arches are part of the skeletal system and hold the gills in place. The first gill arch supports a single row of filaments, and the following four to six gill arches support two rows of filaments each, one attached to each side of a septum. The gill filaments are structured so that water flows one way alongside them, while blood inside the filaments flows in the opposite direction. This countercurrent system efficiently extracts and transports oxygen from the water to the blood and releases carbon dioxide from the blood into the water.

Liver

Primarily a storage depot for carbohydrates and fats, the liver releases sugars such as glycogen into the bloodstream to provide energy as needed. Shark livers also contain oils that help a shark attain neutral buoyancy, and can equal 5% to 30% of a shark's total body weight. A great white shark caught off California's Catalina Island in June 1976 weighed 4,150 pounds, and its liver weighed almost 600 pounds (in contrast, its rela-

The dark-brown, two-lobed liver of a blue shark.

tively small heart weighed just less than ten pounds—slightly more than an average newborn baby).

Deep-sea sharks approach neutral buoyancy by means of a large liver that contains low-density lipids, primarily squalene and dia-cyl glyceryl ether. The relative amounts of these two oils within the liver can change as a shark grows, depending on the animal's

liver

Left: A crocodile shark's large, two-lobed liver provides additional buoyancy.

Center: The cavernous, stretchable stomach of a blue shark.

Bottom: A blue shark can cleanse its stomach in seawater during a process called gastric eversion (preserved, BPBM).

needs. During some periods, the shark might need more or less squalene, which has a lower density and provides more lift. Diacyl glyceryl ether might be needed in abundance at other times. It requires less energy to metabolize and can be used as an energy source.

Unlike human livers, a shark's liver appears to harbor bacteria that break down a potentially toxic urea buildup in the bloodstream.

Stomach

As you might suspect, sharks (and rays, too) have large, flexible stomachs that can expand to hold a great quantity of food. In fact, the stomach can hold up to 13% of the animal's total body weight. Where the stomach is concerned, even researchers studying dead sharks can face dangerous hazards in the course of their work. Strong hydrochloric acid (pH 2.5), which is released when food enters the digestive system, has been known to peel some of the skin from the hands of unwary scientists who come in contact with stomach juices while investigating sharks' dietary habits.

Some sharks also have an interesting habit called gastric eversion. To get rid of unwanted objects that it has swallowed, the shark can push its stomach out through its mouth, turning the stomach inside out during this cleansing process, and then pull it back into the body.

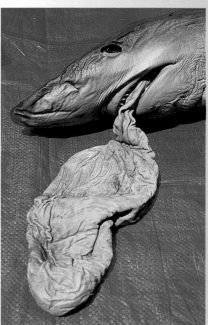

Valvular Intestine

In contrast to most other vertebrates, which have longer and more bulky intestines, sharks and rays typically have short, compact intestines containing one of three types of valves—conicospiral (e.g., shortspine spurdog shark), ring (e.g., crocodile shark) or scroll (e.g., blue shark)—that provide a large amount of surface area in a small space and thus help to increase the absorption of food. In one valvular intestine there may be between 4 and 68 spiral folds (valves), depending on the species.

Sharks with a scroll-valve intestine (all carcharhinids, and hammerheads) can forcibly eject the intestine through the cloaca (lower body opening through which copulation takes place in the female and wastes are expelled) for flushing and cleansing in sea water, then pull it back in to its normal position—a process similar to gastric eversion (see **Stomach** above). Researchers speculate that this intestinal eversion may be a way of removing tapeworm segments or other irritating objects such as squid beaks.

A bigeye thresher shark's ring valve intestine.

The sausage-like scroll valve intestine of the blue shark.

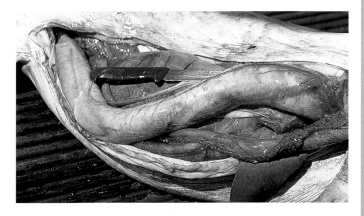

CHAPTER 3

SENSES

Imagine for a moment that you suddenly find yourself in the total darkness of an underground cave. Your eyes are useless in the inky blackness and cannot orient you to the surroundings, so other senses must help you to move around. Your sense of hearing is heightened. The hair on your arms and legs might feel a slight movement of air. Your sense of touch guides you around rocks and along walls.

Sharks and rays, too, must use various senses if they are to orient themselves and search for food in the often formless and dark environs of the ocean. In addition to the five familiar senses (sight, hearing, touch, smell and taste), sharks and rays are also equipped with two additional senses—electroreception and a water-movement sense located in the lateral line canal system— that help them adapt to an aquatic lifestyle, move around, mate, and locate prey.

The electroreception sense in the ampullae of Lorenzini detects electric fields emanating from other animals (and indirectly, the earth's magnetic field). The lateral line picks up water movements. For example, as a fish swims, its body pushes aside the surrounding water, much as waves from the wake of a speedboat spread out across the water's surface. When detected by the lateral line, these water movements provide information such as the size, swimming speed and location of the moving fish. The lateral line, hearing and touch senses are called mechano-sensory, because they all make use of receptors that respond to contact with a mechanical stimulus such as water or another physical object.

The acronym SOVLETT can help us remember these senses and show us the order (from far to near) a shark might encounter stimuli as it approaches an object. The letters stand for **S**ound, **O**lfaction (smell), **V**ision, **L**ateral line, **E**lectroreception (ampullae of Lorenzini), **T**ouch, and **T**aste. Each of these senses will be discussed in this chapter.

*With their ampullae of Lorenzini, spotted
eagle rays can sense the earth's magnetic field.*

Jack Randall

An active, foraging shark like this gray reef can hear sounds from a hundred yards away.

Sound

The ocean can be a very noisy environment. Because sound travels almost five times faster in water than in air, a multitude of sounds—from shrimp snapping and parrotfish crunching on coral, to rocks colliding in the wave zone—can be very distracting, so sharks and rays must tune out all these extraneous noises if they are to listen for the sounds made by wounded fish or other potential prey.

Sharks' and rays' inner ears are encased in the chondrocranium (skull), and sound waves reach these organs through two small pores on top of the head. Inside the inner ear, three semicircular canals and three nodules (utriculus, lagena and sacculus) affect orientation and balance; and a tiny structure in the sacculus called the macula neglecta—the actual hearing center—contains nerve and hair cells, both of which respond to sound vibrations. These vibrating hair cells indicate the direction a sound is coming from.

As might be expected, hair cells in active, foraging sharks are more numerous and cover a wider area than hair cells in bottom-feeding rays. It has been estimated that a shark can hear directional sounds from 100 yards away (the length of a football field) and its hearing appears to be more acute at about 20-300 Hz— the low-frequency range of a struggling fish. Researchers have noted that low-frequency pulsed sounds from a recorder attract sharks, who mill about or bump the speaker looking for potential prey. If sharks are not fed when they respond to the playback sound, they become habituated to the sound and learn to ignore it. Eventually, no experienced shark will be attracted to the previously inviting sound.

Olfaction

Both sharks and rays have a well-developed sense of smell, which plays a role in feeding and locating a mate. Each of two nostrils, located underneath the snout between the snout tip and the upper jaw, is aligned to allow water to flow in one side of the nostril and out the other. This creates a pressure difference that forces odors over the nostrils' sensory folds and past mucus and cilia, which detect even minute concentrations of these smells—perhaps as minute as one part per billion. In other words, when it comes to smell, sharks and rays are able to find that olfactory needle in a haystack.

Some sharks have been observed swimming in an "S" pattern while trying to locate the source of an odor. Each directional, back-and-forth turn in this search pattern leads the shark down an olfactory corridor. In tests, lemon sharks following an olfactory "S" pattern swam past the source of the smell (an invisible odor discharged from a hidden pipe), indicating that once they get close to a potential food source, they rely on other senses in an attempt to locate it. Similar tests showed that nurse sharks did not use an "S" pattern. They turned into the current and swam directly to the source of the smell.

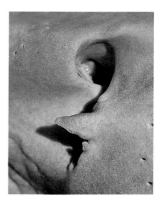

Vision

Sharks have eyes on the sides of their heads. These eyes are far enough apart that they probably do not function with binocular vision (as human eyes do) in which both eyes are used together to focus on an object. In addition to well-developed eyelids that don't completely cover the eyeball, some shark species have a nictitating membrane that covers the eye to prevent damage, particularly during feeding. Other sharks roll their eyes into the eye socket (and away from the eye opening) for protection.

A crocodile shark has no nictitating membrane but can roll its eye into the eye socket for protection.

The anatomy of a shark's eye is similar to that of a human: It has a cornea, lens, iris, retina, and the vitreous humor (a transparent chamber of jelly) behind the lens but in front of the retina. The retina of sharks and rays studied to date contains rods and cones, which provide visual sharpness and the potential for color vision. In sharks and rays, however, the white area of the eye (the sclera) is supported by cartilage, rather than bone. Also in sharks and rays (but not in humans), the choroid or nutritive layer of the eye contains the tapetum lucidum—a layer of cells behind the retina that makes efficient use of light by reflecting it back through the rods of the retina a second time. If the headlights of your car have ever caught the eyes of a cat or dog at night, you've seen this mirror-like reflection at work. It helps certain animals see extremely well in low light conditions.

Many sharks hunt near the sunlit surface of the ocean. To prevent their eyes from being overstimulated by this bright light, these sharks have adapted in a unique way: Dark pigments migrate over the tapetum lucidum to adjust the amount of light reaching the retina. Also, the pupil is capable of dilating and contracting. It can change its opening size by a factor of ten as the shark swims from bright light to darkness and vice versa.

The nictitating membrane protects a blue shark's eye during feeding.

Even sharks can blink—a whitetip reef shark reacts to the camera flash by covering its eye with a nictitating membrane.

The lens of a shark's eye is hard and thick, unlike a thin and flexible human eye lens.

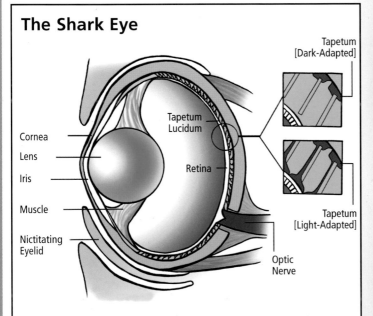

The Shark Eye

Tapetum
[Dark-Adapted]

Tapetum
Lucidum

Cornea

Lens

Retina

Iris

Muscle

Tapetum
[Light-Adapted]

Nictitating
Eyelid

Optic
Nerve

*Left: The Shark Eye.
Illustration by
Audra Furuichi.*

The mirror-like tapetum lucidum in the eye reflects light.

While the lens of the human eye is thin and elastic, and can be stretched for distance vision and relaxed for near vision, the lens in the eye of a shark or ray is hard and thick and cannot stretch. It must adjust for far and near vision by moving forward or backward in the eye socket using muscle and ligament tension. Sharks don't all have the same type of lens, and some may be able to focus more effectively than others. Also, the lens of one shark—the lemon shark—has seven times more focusing power than the human eye. This shark's retina contains a dense horizontal band of cones and ganglion cells called a visual streak, which is thought to provide better visual sharpness than a more scattered assortment of cells. Such a visual streak might provide sharp, concentrated vision along a narrow band of sight for sharks living in shallow water where most visual targets appear from side to side, rather than above or below.

The green eye of a deep-sea bluntnose sixgill shark.

While the retina of coastal sharks contains a purple pigment, the retinal pigment color in deep-sea sharks is blue, which responds to the dim, blue-green light in the ocean's depths and the greenish glow produced by bioluminescent organisms. The tiger shark lens contains a yellow pigment that could function as a UV filter or help enhance upward vision into bright surface light. From the research to date, it seems clear that different species of sharks and rays living in a myriad of diverse locations have adapted their remarkable eyesight to the needs of their specific environments.

A bigeye thresher shark can see objects above its head as well as on both sides.

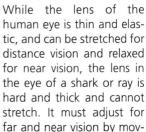

The lateral line of a blue shark.

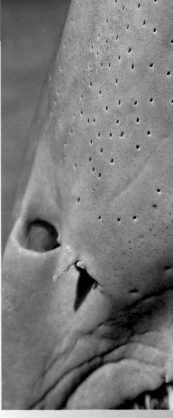

Lateral Line

The lateral line is composed of a series of connected canals that run under the skin, around the head, along both sides of the body and into the tail. A series of pores penetrate through the skin and allow saltwater to flow into the canal system, where specialized cells called neuromasts can detect changes in water motion from about one to two body lengths away. When these water-motion changes reach the neuromasts, they activate nerve impulses to the brain, providing information that helps the animal better interpret its environment. This might include helping the shark or ray to locate food since the lateral line can feel very small, jerky waves made by injured fish. The lateral line also allows a shark or ray to feel the waves its own body makes while swimming.

Pores scattered around a sand tiger's jaw and snout lead to the ampullae of Lorenzini (preserved, BPBM).

A bigeye thresher's prominent lateral line.

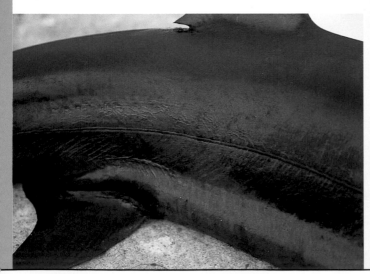

In addition, pit organs, which contain neuromasts (not part of the lateral line canal system) are scattered on a shark's skin between the scales. The number of pit organs on the side of the body can range from about 70 in the piked dogfish shark to more than 600 in the scalloped hammerhead. These structures detect the movement of water, and possibly its speed, over the skin. Both the pit organs and the lateral line can detect water currents and provide information about other animals—prey and predator—swimming nearby.

Electroreception
(Ampullae of Lorenzini)

Sharks and rays have a sense that only two land animals (the duckbilled platypus and the echidna [spiny anteater]) and very few other fish have. All living organisms generate a weak electric field around their bodies. Sensory pores around the eyes, lower jaw and snout can tell the shark or ray exactly where these electric fields are coming from. This sense, called electroreception (ampullae of Lorenzini), works almost like a metal detector to locate fish buried in sand. Even if a fish is not moving, the ampullae can detect its electric field at close range.

Ampullae of Lorenzini pores pattern this silky shark's snout.

Each ampulla (electroreceptive organ) contains nerve fibers and consists of a pore at the surface of the skin and a canal filled with gel that leads from the pore to the ampulla. Increasing the electric field intensity around a shark or ray causes these nerve fibers to fire more rapidly. Shark repellent devices such as the shark stick or POD (more about these in **Chapter 12**) make use of this rapid firing mechanism to overload the ampullae with a strong electrical charge that often repels the shark.

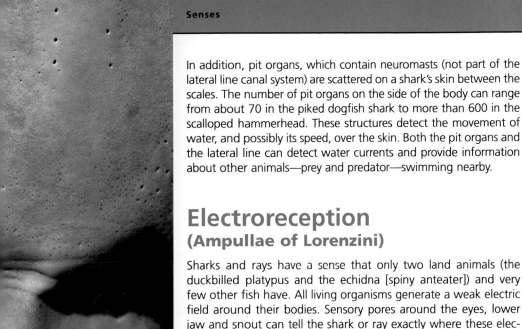

These sensitive nerve fibers—they have detected electrical fields as low as 5 nanovolts (one nanovolt equals a billionth of a volt)—might be used to find the earth's magnetic field for traveling short distances or even for long-distance migration. Researchers observing hammerhead sharks in the Gulf of California postulated that the sharks were sensing changes in the earth's magnetic field and using geomagnetic electrical intensity as a positioning device to navigate to and from a seamount.

Like a mine sweeper, a hammerhead swings its wide head over the sandy sea floor searching for buried food with its electrical-field sensory system.

Eagle rays have a well-developed sense of touch.

Biting responses can be triggered by buried cables that carry an electric charge and by the weaker electric field produced by metal cages or boats. Television crews often attract sharks by chumming or hanging a dead fish below the boat. The shark's excellent sense of smell will draw it to the source of potential food, but at close range, when sharks open their mouths to bite, they rely on the ampullae of Lorenzini to guide them the last foot or so to their meal. Dead fish don't put out an electric field, but metal in sea water does, so the shark will often end up blindly biting the cage or boat—following the electric impulses.

To test a sharks' responses to odors and electroreception, researcher Ad Kalmijn attracted sharks with herring juice then observed their reactions to a nearby electrode. Although the dogfish and blue sharks in the study were initially attracted by the odor, most of them veered off at the last second to bite the electrode, showing the importance of electroreception in feeding behavior. Under most circumstances, sharks that were originally attracted by a smell, will ignore that smell at close range and bite or bump the source of the electric field.

Electroreception may also be useful for detecting predators and mates at close range.

Touch

Much like human skin, the skin of sharks and rays is equipped with a well-developed sense of touch—on the head, body and fins.

Taste

A bigeye thresher's tongue is covered with taste buds.

Taste buds, inside small, finger-like protrusions that project slightly from the skin lining, are found on the tongue, the lining of the mouth and the pharynx. These very sensitive organs can detect minute chemical concentrations. In fact, in one study conducted to determine how sharks react to different kinds of food, the discerning sharks spat out squid treated with alcohol.

CHAPTER 4

FEEDING HABITS

No matter what they do, sharks can't win. A shark captured with its stomach full of food is branded a glutton. And if caught with an empty stomach, the shark must be hunting for its next victim, satisfying a never-ending urge to eat.

Actually, a shark eats less than you might think. Juvenile sandbar sharks, for example, consume an estimated 1% of their body weight per day— that's just under one ounce of food a day for a 5-pound young-ster (the equivalent of us eating about a dozen crackers). Because adult sharks no longer need energy for rapid growth, they eat even less—only half of one percent of their body weight per day (just under one pound a day for a 5-foot female sandbar shark weighing 190 pounds). Sharks, however, can't visit a handy grocery store every day and often go for a week or more without feeding.

Perhaps because of these and other reasons, sharks digest their food at a slower rate than do bony fish (digestion rates vary depending on water temperature and food type—in a shark's stomach, fish digest faster than crunchy crustaceans). Studies show that in the lemon shark *(Negaprion brevirostris)*, a meal takes about 68 to 82 hours to digest, whereas when bony fish eat a meal, it digests in only 50 hours at a similar temperature. For tropical sharks living in warm water, the time needed for a meal to clear the stomach ranges from 28 to 92 hours. But the spiny dogfish shark *(Squalus acanthias)*, which inhabits colder waters, requires 124 hours.

Left page: Fish scatter when two Galapagos sharks approach.

Above—inset: Crocodile sharks feed on crustaceans, squid, shrimp and bony fish.

Right: A juvenile sandbar shark searches for food in Kāne'ohe Bay.

No matter what the water temperature, some unusual things found in sharks' stomachs might be more difficult or impossible to digest: automobile license plates, a sack of coal, deer horns, a chicken coop, the head and forequarters of a crocodile, parts of hippos and elephants, and even a complete suit of armor.

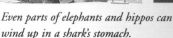

Even parts of elephants and hippos can wind up in a shark's stomach.

True Tales

Some unusual shark stomach contents once appeared as evidence in a court of law. In 1799 when the United States and Britain were at war, the British cutter, HMS *Sparrow*, part of the British Navy's blockade of Haiti, spotted and chased Captain Thomas Briggs' American brigantine, *Nancy*. To conceal the ship's American identity before she was boarded, Briggs threw the vessel's identification papers (tied in string) overboard. During the court proceedings in Port Royale, Jamaica, a ship's captain presented the missing papers as evidence after he found them in a captured shark's stomach. As a result, the American ship and her cargo became a lawful prize of war. The infamous 'shark papers' are still on display at the Institute of Jamaica in Kingston.

In an unusual case of shark mail, a shark was captured with a bottle in its stomach. The bottle contained a letter from a dying French fisherman whose boat had sunk. From his life raft, he had written the farewell note to his wife and children and thrown it overboard in the bottle.

Perhaps the most gruesome story tells of a human arm preserved in the stomach of a shark off the coast of Australia. On cutting open the shark, the fisherman noticed a smaller shark in its stomach. Inside the smaller shark, which had apparently died before strong digestive acids could dissolve its stomach contents, he discovered a muscular arm—deliberately sliced off at the shoulder with a butcher's knife. Authorities identified the victim— an amateur boxer—by a tattoo on the forearm and by recreating the withered fingerprints. Unfortunately, they never located the rest of the victim and lacked enough evidence to prosecute the suspected killer.

Great white sharks are ambush predators.

Amos Nachoum/Innerspace Visions

Above: Like most sharks, a whitetip reef won't pass up an easy meal.

Feeding Behavior

As a rule, sharks feed alone, a fact that contrasts with the many feeding-frenzy images on television—most of which are contrived and unnatural situations, the result of dive-boat operators or camera crews providing an overstimulating sound, visual or food attraction.

Some sharks do congregate with other sharks during the day and then separate at night, moving off to more widespread, individual feeding areas. Other species feed at different depths, migrating hundreds of feet from the surface to deeper waters and back again on a daily basis.

The whitetip reef shark rests in underwater caves during the day, venturing out on its feeding forays at night. However, no matter what the time of day, this clever shark has learned how to pick off an easy meal. When it hears a boat near its resting area, the whitetip reef will come out of its cave and steal speared fish from divers.

The great white, like most sharks, is an ambush predator, approaching prey from below or behind, a technique similar to that exploited by the African lion. But unlike most sharks studied, the great white appears to hunt during the day, taking advantage of the sun to silhouette marine mammals as it swims beneath them.

Some sharks might capitalize on their bioluminescence to attract prey. As a means of luring larger fish to a potential meal, parts of the diminutive cookiecutter shark glow a bioluminescent green. Then, when a large predator gets close enough, the aggressive cookiecutter turns and becomes the attacker, sawing a golf-ball-sized chunk from the flesh of its surprised pursuer.

Cynthia Vanderlip

This Hawaiian monk seal at Midway Atoll survived a run-in with a shark.

Camouflage, too, can be employed as a hunting technique. While the grayish brown body of an oceanic whitetip blends into its formless surroundings, the visible white splotches on its fins might confuse nearby fish and cause them to mistake the markings for other silvery fish in the dim light. Countershading (dark on top, light underneath) is a form of camouflage. Viewed from above, the great white's dark dorsal surface blends in with the dark sea floor, making it harder for seals and sea lions above to see the shark in time to escape. Seen from below, the shark's white underbelly blends in with the sunlit ocean surface.

We know that sharks hunt for prey in a variety of ways. However, we have a lot to learn in this area because the feeding behavior of most sharks has yet to be studied.

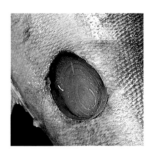

Above: Cookiecutter sharks leave their distinctive bite marks on large prey like this tuna at Honolulu's fish auction.

Below: White fin splotches stand out on an oceanic whitetip shark.

Tom Fenske

*Right: Kāne'ohe Bay
serves as a nursery
area for scalloped
hammerhead pups.*

*Below: A scalloped
hammerhead pup.*

Separate Feeding Areas

Many shark species gravitate to specific nursery feeding areas where juveniles are separated from adults. This segregation provides a safe, suitable habitat that often reduces competition for food, allows juveniles to hone their hunting skills, and helps prevent adult sharks from preying on young sharks as they grow.

In the case of the scalloped hammerhead, pregnant females choose shallow, protected inlets like Kāne'ohe Bay for their pupping grounds, then move offshore to adult areas after the young are born. In Kāne'ohe Bay, food for juvenile scalloped hammerheads consists primarily of benthic (bottom-dwelling) shrimp and goby fish. Adults eat mostly fish, pelagic squid and stingrays.

The Hawaiian sandbar shark population also appears to be segregated, not by location but by depth, at least part of the year. Fishing records indicate that adult males are caught at an average depth of 367 feet, juveniles at 260 feet, and adult females at 223 feet. Biologists don't know why this segregation takes place (Could it be related to diet, fewer predators for the young sharks, or an equally compelling reason?) or how long juveniles and adults remain in their separate areas. They believe, however, that males enter the female depth range during mating season.

Jack Randall

Sandbar shark.

Left: These tiger shark jaws and teeth are made for eating just about anything.

Bottom Left: Tiger sharks cruise Midway Atoll's lagoon during June and July—albatross fledgling season.

Below: A tiger shark lunges for a Laysan albatross.

Jack Randall

Cynthia Vanderlip

Chad Yoshinaga, NMFS

What's For Dinner?

The amount and type of food eaten often varies with a shark's age. In Hawai'i, juvenile tiger sharks (smaller than 6.5 feet) feed primarily on bony fish (89%), birds (22%) and cephalopods such as octopi and squid (17%). Subadult tigers (6.5 to 9.8 feet) consume a wider variety of prey that includes bony fish (78%), crustaceans (32%), birds (20%), rays and other sharks (20%), land mammals (19%), cephalopods (16%) and sea turtles (7%).

Adult tiger sharks (longer than 9.8 feet) eat a large number of rays and other sharks (42%), bony fish (40%), crustaceans (35%), birds (25%), land mammals (19%), sea turtles (15%), cephalopods (10%) and marine mammals (7%). It's clear that as tiger sharks grow, they devour a wider variety of prey and can feed on larger and more challenging species.

Table Manners

In addition to differences in shark hunting strategies and feeding behaviors, a look at the varieties of shark teeth (see **Chapter 2: Anatomy**) confirms the fact that sharks don't all eat the same

Above: Say Aaaaah! When feeding, whale sharks swim with their mouths wide open.

way. In fact, their range of feeding specializations is truly remarkable. Large filter-feeding whale sharks, megamouth sharks and manta rays employ gill rakers to remove food from the water. The cookiecutter shark—considered a functional parasite—carves tissue plugs from its much-larger victims. To dine on food buried in sand, the spotted eagle ray relies on its electrical-sensory system (ampullae of Lorenzini) and flexible beak-like snout to locate and capture prey it cannot see. The hammerhead shark, too, finds hidden prey by maneuvering its wide head back and forth, in mine-sweeper fashion, a few inches from the ocean floor. A thresher shark uses its elongated tail to encircle and trap a school of fish. And bioluminescence and distinctive markings can also make up part of an animal's food-gathering arsenal.

Opposite Page: The fearless cookiecutter shark takes bites out of animals much larger than itself.

Right: Cookiecutter bite in the flesh of a Hawaiian monk seal.

Now let's take a look at some unique and highly effective shark and ray dining strategies and the types of utensils (teeth) used in the process.

Filter Feeders

This group includes the reclusive megamouth shark. Since the megamouth has never been observed feeding in its natural habitat, biologists must piece together information about its filtering strategy by studying the few specimens accidentally caught and now preserved in museums. Their research has resulted in the following conclusions: Swimming slowly through a swarm of its prey—euphausiid shrimp—with its mouth slightly ajar, the megamouth suddenly thrusts open its wide jaws, and the strong suction pulls millions of tiny shrimp into the cavernous orifice. Pressure forces the inhaled sea water out through the gill slits, but the shrimp are trapped on strainer-like gill rakers. Researchers also think that shrimp and other small prey might be drawn to the silvery, luminescent tissue inside this shark's mouth.

A bigeye thresher's whip-like tail is used in food gathering.

Mark Dell'Aquila

The rare, filter-feeding megamouth uses suction and gill rakers to gather food.

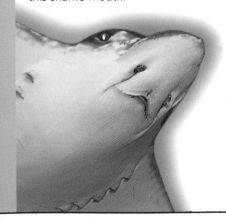

The spotted eagle ray's pointed snout helps it dig for food in the sandy sea floor.

Manta ray gill rakers (below pencil) (preserved, BPBM).

Spinetail devil ray gill rakers.

Print courtesy of Mauna Kea Beach Hotel.

Above: Graceful manta rays can be seen feeding at night from the Mauna Kea Beach Hotel's oceanside terrace.

Left: Whale baleen performs the same function as shark and ray gill rakers—straining food.

Below: An open-mouthed manta ray (Lefty) feeds amidst a swarm of plankton—its favorite food.

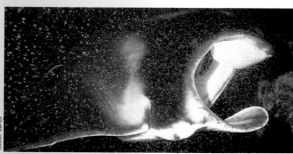

Keller Laros

Also a filter feeder, the graceful manta ray can be seen at night from the seaside terrace of the Mauna Kea Beach Hotel on the Big Island of Hawai'i. Attracted to swarms of minuscule crustaceans, which are, in turn, lured by the hotel's bright lights (and occasionally the underwater lights of divers swimming with the rays), the mantas swim in barrel-loop, 360-degree circles again and again, their wide mouths inhaling the congregated crustaceans, to the delight of their audience.

The whale shark, another filter feeder, occasionally breaks the surface of the water, where fish jump into its open mouth. Filter-feeding sharks and rays do have teeth in addition to their gill rakers, but these minuscule teeth perform no function during feeding.

Manta ray teeth (dots, above) are no bigger than the tip of a pencil point.

Pat Kesling-Wood

A tuna on the line is no guarantee of a tuna in the boat when there are hungry sharks hanging around.

Pat Kesling-Wood

Above: A Galapagos shark at Midway Atoll zeros in on a chunk of tuna.

Right: A blue shark's serrated, knife-like teeth.

Gouging Teeth

In general, sharks with gouging teeth feed in the following way: When a shark approaches its victim, it slows down by lowering the trailing edges of its large pectoral fins (much as an aileron is lowered on the back edge of an aircraft wing). This action also lifts the head and front part of the shark (again, much like a plane when it lands on the runway). Muscles at the back of the neck region tighten to open the mouth and lift the snout, allowing the teeth of the lower jaw to impale the prey. When the prey is secure, the upper teeth are thrust forward and outward and begin a sawing action powered by violent side-to-side swings of the shark's head and forebody.

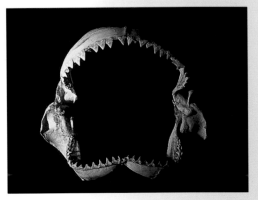

Above: An oceanic whitetip shark's gouging teeth.

Below: These pointed, spear-like teeth belong to a whitetip reef shark.

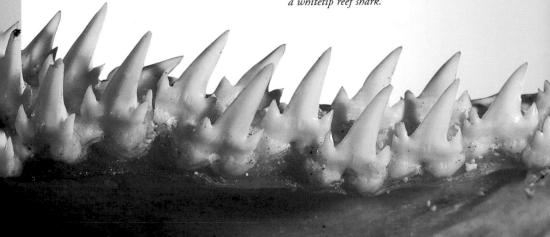

Right: With a powerful body and dagger-like teeth in both upper and lower jaws, the mako easily catches its prey.

John Buchanan, NMFS-PIAO

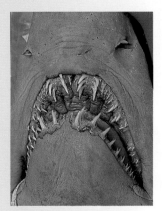

A sand tiger's teeth make it look ferocious, but this mellow shark eats mainly fish (preserved, BPBM).

A juvenile silky shark shows off a knife-like set of teeth.

This juvenile bigeye thresher shark's grabbing teeth will widen as they mature.

Gordon Hubbell

Tiny cusplets flank a juvenile great white shark's narrow upper-jaw teeth.

Gordon Hubbell

Cusplets disappear by the time a great white reaches adulthood.

The teeth of many carcharhinid (sandbar, Galapagos, tiger) and lamnid (great white) sharks grab and gouge chunks out of prey. Typically, the lower jaw teeth are more slender and pointed (for grabbing), while the upper jaw teeth are broader and serrated (for cutting and gouging). Great white teeth effortlessly slice through large marine mammals, and tiger shark teeth saw through sea-turtle shells with relative ease.

The mako shark's dagger-like teeth, adapted for grabbing, holding and swallowing prey whole, also belong to this group.

A juvenile shark may display different tooth development than an adult. Great white adults, for example, show off broad, stand-alone teeth, while the narrower teeth of a juvenile great white are each flanked by two cusplets (tiny, pointed teeth at the base of the main tooth). Since juveniles feed heavily on fish, and adults hunt marine mammals, tooth shape might be related to diet.

Suction/ Crushing Teeth

Stingrays and eagle rays have small mouths. This feature, combined with an expandable pharyngeal cavity (a type of muscular throat area) creates a vacuum that sucks in small bottom-dwelling organisms. The movable upper jaw, which, as in sharks, is not firmly attached to the brain case, helps to direct suction currents into the ray's stomach.

As we mentioned earlier, because of their abundant ampullae of Lorenzini, rays can detect prey hiding in a sandy sea floor. Locating prey is one thing, but retrieving it is another. Eagle rays, however, are perfectly adapted for this process. By jetting streams of water through their mouths, they can blast away the sand to get at their prey. During low tide, cylindrical sand depressions—sometimes as much as ten inches wide and deep—are visible in eagle ray feeding areas.

An eagle ray uses its specialized, flat, pavement-like teeth for breaking up shelled food such as crustaceans and clams. Shells, once crushed, are spit out, and the food sucked into the throat and swallowed. The somewhat flattened teeth of dasyatid stingrays also break up food, but this group owns a quirky tooth-shape distinction: Male teeth are more pointed than female teeth, possibly allowing a male to bite and hold on to his partner's body during mating. This difference allows observers to determine the sex of these stingrays just by looking at their teeth.

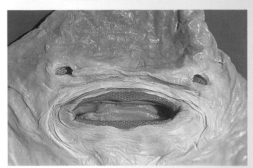

An sixgill stingray's muscular throat sucks food into its small mouth (preserved, BPBM).

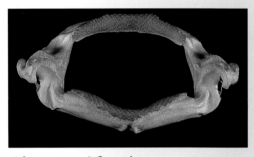

A brown stingray's flat teeth.

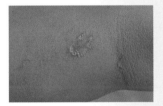

A brown stingray's smooth-looking teeth can raise a welt on an aquarist's leg.

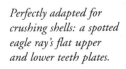

Perfectly adapted for crushing shells: a spotted eagle ray's flat upper and lower teeth plates.

The sharp teeth of a male pelagic (dasyatid) stingray.

Cutting Teeth

In the shortspine spurdog, both upper and lower-jaw teeth are low and sharp (like tiny razor blades) and tightly overlapped to form a continuous knife edge that runs from one side of the mouth to the other. These cutting teeth easily slice up prey such as squid and bony fish into bite-size pieces.

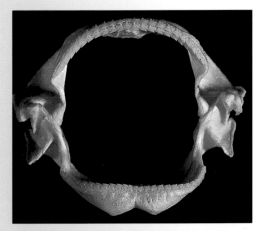

Other sharks come equipped with an unusual combination of grabbing and cutting teeth. Lantern sharks (genus *Etmopterus*) have well-developed cutting teeth in their lower jaws as well as an upper-jaw tooth-shape sexual variation: more-pointed, grabbing teeth (and more cusplets beside each tooth) in mature males compared to females—possibly, as with rays, to hold on to their partners during mating.

Little by little, researchers are gaining a better understanding of the feeding habits of sharks and rays. We now know, for example, that they are opportunistic hunters who take advantage of prey whenever it is available. We've also learned that they usually feed in cycles, at times actively foraging for food, followed by lengthy periods of digestion when little feeding activity takes place. Sharks, in particular, once thought to be incessant eating machines, are losing their "swimming stomach" image and becoming more understood as an integral part of the ocean's food web.

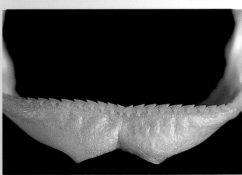

Top: Shortspine spurdog shark jaw and teeth.

Center: The cutting lower-jaw teeth of a shortspine spurdog shark.

Bottom: Lantern sharks have both lower-jaw cutting teeth and an upper jaw filled with multi-cusped grabbing teeth.

During mating, a whitetip reef shark bites his partner's pectoral fin (inset at right) before inserting a clasper into her cloaca (above).

CHAPTER 5

SEX LIVES OF SHARKS AND RAYS

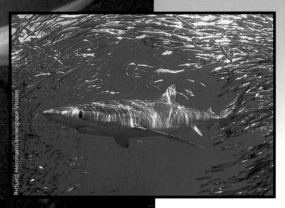

Inset above: North Pacific blue sharks mate near Hawai'i.

Richard Herrmann/Innerspace Visions

Eric M. Le Feuvre

Different Strokes for Different Sharks

Sharks do not form pair bonds and usually come together only when they're ready to mate. Since some of Hawai'i's sharks inhabit or give birth to their pups in the coastal areas around islands, and others spend most of their lives in the pelagic waters of the open ocean, they often show different types of reproductive patterns. Coastal-pupping sharks, such as the scalloped hammerhead, give birth seasonally (May-July). Pelagic species such as the oceanic whitetip, silky, pelagic thresher, bigeye thresher and frilled sharks, on the other hand, apparently reproduce year-round—embryos of different sizes have been found at all times of the year. The blue shark, although pelagic, is thought to mate and pup every two years.

The blue shark in the North Pacific inhabits virtually the entire region from the Aleutian Islands in the north to a distance of 4,200 miles south, and 9,000 miles from east to west. A vast area indeed, yet blues congregate in very specific yet separate areas at certain times of year depending on the abundance or lack of food, their age group, and the reproductive season.

When it's time to mate, male and female North Pacific blue sharks know instinctively where to find each other. Just like typical honeymooners, they head for Hawai'i, or at least to a broad band of ocean in the general vicinity of the Hawaiian Island chain. After mating, pregnant females migrate north—to an area in the open ocean at roughly the same latitude as Eureka, California, where they give birth to their pups in May and June. Then they head south, while pups stay in their northern food-abundant nursery areas for four to six years before traveling south to join their respective adult populations. Except during mating season, adult male blue sharks tend to stay at the southern end of their Pacific territory. Females range throughout a wider area but usually further north than males.

Very little is known about the mating behavior of stingrays around Hawai'i except for the brown stingrays of Kāne'ohe Bay. Both males and females of this species remain year-round in the bay and only express sexual interest in each other during the summer mating season.

Courtship Rituals

Although sharks and rays know where their species' mating grounds are, it would be easy for males and females to miss each other even in coastal areas without an additional clue. Luckily there is such a clue: Females send out chemical signals called pheromones, which can be picked up from some distance away. This species-specific odor trail lets the male know when a female is ready for mating and where to find her.

When a male shark reaches an available female, they may at first swim, nose to tail, in tight clockwise circles—he following her chemical scent—a behavior observed in basking sharks. Male sharks have a curious and aggressive approach to courtship. After repeatedly prodding and pushing against the female with increasing force, a behavior lasting from an hour or two in some species to days in others, they repeatedly bite their mates on the flanks, back, tail, pectoral fins and around the gill openings, leaving tooth nicks, slashes and semicircular jaw impressions on her skin. In an effort to compensate for this deliberate mauling, nature has endowed some female sharks—the blue in particular—with thick skin—at least twice as thick as males.

Mating bite marks on a pregnant crocodile shark.

Biting stimulates the female to copulate. In some coastal sharks, when the frenzied male realizes his partner is ready, he bites and holds on to one of her pectoral fins with his teeth, anchoring the pair together during copulation. Pelagic sharks may follow the same pattern, but most have not been seen during the mating ritual. However, in one instance, researchers did observe a pair of scalloped hammerheads locked in a mating embrace in the Gulf of California off the coast of the Baja peninsula. Oblivious to their surroundings, they sank to the rocky top of a seamount before separating.

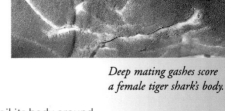

Courtesy of the Waikiki Aquarium.

Deep mating gashes score a female tiger shark's body.

In some smaller, flexible species, the male can coil its body around the female as a way of keeping the pair together and in the correct position. With the larger, stiffer-bodied sharks, coiling is not likely, so mating couples must swim side by side while the male inserts his clasper and injects the sperm.

Spotted eagle rays follow a similar courtship ritual during which the smaller male bites the trailing edge of the female's wing, then rotates into a belly-to-belly position and inserts a clasper. According to observers watching captive spotted eagle rays, this procedure lasts about one minute.

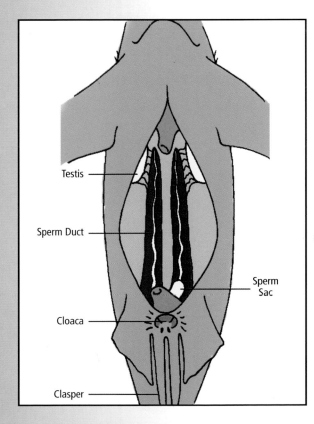

Testis

Sperm Duct

Cloaca

Clasper

Sperm Sac

Male Reproductive System— Bundles of Sperm

As do many animal species, male sharks produce sperm in a paired reproductive gland—the testis. Because this sperm has some unique obstacles to overcome before it fertilizes the female ovum, sharks have developed an ingenious method of protecting their sperm during its perilous journey. This method is called bundling.

Sperm are produced in one of two ways. In radial testes, found in lamnid sharks such as makos and great whites, sperm originate in the centers of a number of circular follicles and then migrate toward the follicle edges much in the way that the spokes of a bicycle wheel radiate from the hub to the rim. In the second method, diametric testes (the carcharhinid group: blue, oceanic whitetip, silky), sperm are formed at an elongated seam—the germinal zone—on one side of the testes, then spread out, fanlike, toward the opposite side.

Once the sperm leave the testes through hair-sized tubes called efferent ductules and travel along the ductus deferens—a long, highly coiled tube in mature sharks—a sticky, mucous-like substance clumps them together into bundles called spermatozeugmata.

When the bundled spermatozeugmata reach a storage bag, the seminal vesicle, they look a lot like grains of rice—small grains in some species such as the shortfin mako shark, and larger grains in the basking shark. Biologists think the sticky mucous protects the spermatozeugmata from disintegrating while they travel along the male's clasper groove into the female—a hazardous trip that exposes the sperm bundles to sea water.

Top: Claspers are stiff extensions of the pelvic fins.

Center: The tip of a blue shark's clasper expands to anchor it inside a female during mating.

Bottom: The shortspine spurdog shark's clasper spine keeps a mating pair from separating before sperm is transferred.

The Clasper Connection

Male sharks have two cigar-shaped external reproductive organs called claspers, but only one is inserted into the female during mating. These claspers—extensions of the pelvic fins—are visible in embryonic sharks and grow rapidly during puberty, becoming noticeably stiffer, thicker and stronger just before the shark reaches sexual maturity and then ceasing to grow any further, even as the shark's body continues to grow. For this reason, older male sharks appear to have relatively smaller claspers than their younger mature relatives.

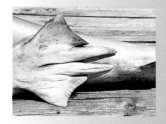

Mating is a vigorous and energetic proposition wherever sharks live, but more so in the open ocean where the pair must continue to swim while copulating. To keep the inserted clasper from being yanked out of the female during the encounter, it is equipped with one of two locking devices. In some sharks a spur or spine on the outer tip of the clasper secures it inside the female. In other species, the blue shark for example, multiple grooves on the tip become thicker or fan out—much like a wall-mounting anchor or toggle bolt—holding the clasper in place during the tumultuous mating process. Accidents do happen, even to sharks, and some males have been found with only one clasper—the other one apparently torn off during or at the conclusion of mating.

Located on the interior edges of the pelvic fins, each clasper transfers sperm into the female via a groove or channel running along its exterior length. This channel is not a completely closed passageway, although its edges usually overlap. Sperm bundles must,

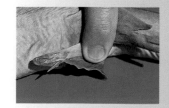

Juvenile male silky shark claspers and cloaca.

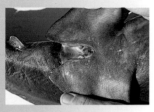

A female bigeye thresher shark's cloaca.

in effect, cross a few micrometers of open ocean to reach it since there is no internal duct to carry them safely from the cloaca—the urogenital opening in a shark's abdomen—to the clasper channel. For the sperm, crossing this tiny chasm is a bit like a spark zapping across the gap between points on a spark plug.

Only part of the clasper is inserted into the female, and the procedure requires a good deal of flexibility on the part of the male. While swimming side by side with his mate, he must bend his stiff appendage across his body so that its groove comes into contact with the urogenital papilla in his cloaca. Spermatozeugmata are ejected from their holding area, the seminal vesicle, through the cloaca and into the clasper groove.

To help the sperm bundles pass along the groove into the female, seawater is first sucked into the male's muscular siphon sac by a process known as clasper flexion—a sideways pumping action of the clasper before it is inserted into the female. Then, during mating and sperm ejection, the siphon sac forcibly expels this water into the clasper groove, carrying most of the sperm along the groove and into the female's uterus. Here, uterine contractions shunt the sperm to the female storage facility—the oviducal gland. According to prevailing knowledge, these uterine contractions are aided by the chemical serotonin, which is also carried in the river of water and produced by the siphon sac. Inevitably, some sperm is lost at sea during its journey.

Rays, too, mate using claspers but don't have a siphon sac filled with sea water. Instead, a clasper gland at the base of the clasper secretes a dense, syrupy fluid containing proteins and lipids. Researchers don't know much about this secretion but think it may help to lubricate and seal the clasper groove, preventing some loss of sperm during mating.

Female Reproductive System

Most sharks in Hawai'i have only one functional ovary (blue, sandbar, Galapagos and tiger sharks use the right ovary; rays use the left. In the frilled shark, both ovaries produce eggs). Ovaries release mature eggs directly into the body cavity where hair-like cilia on the liver and other organs move them into the ostium, a funnel-like organ that shunts them into the oviduct. On their journey to the uterus, which is an enlarged section of the oviduct, they pass through the oviducal gland. If both uteri are being used (the frilled shark uses only the right; spotted eagle rays and stingrays, the left) the ostium appears to act like a Y-shaped conveyer belt, directing eggs alternatively to the left and right oviducal glands and uteri. Once in the multi-purpose oviducal gland, eggs are not only fertilized, but also sheathed in a protective covering or wrapper.

For days (thresher shark), months (blue shark) or sometimes up to a year (scalloped hammerhead), sperm deposited during mating is stored in the oviducal gland waiting for the eggs to arrive. Sperm storage gives the female time for her journey to feeding grounds where she can fill up on nutrients in preparation for egg development and further travel to pupping grounds.

Instead of storing sperm, the diamond stingray, studied in Mexico, fertilizes eggs shortly after mating, then holds them in limbo (embryonic diapause) for nine months before they start to develop. Pupping takes place only three months later, during summer when food for the young rays is abundant.

Mounting evidence—more than one male shark's sperm in storage and the resultant genetically different pups in a single uterus—suggests that each female mates with more than one male during a given mating season. This strategy might give sharks an evolutionary advantage, producing pups that are fitter and more adaptable to changing and harsh environments. Research done in this area so far has been limited to the lemon shark, a non-Hawaiian coastal species.

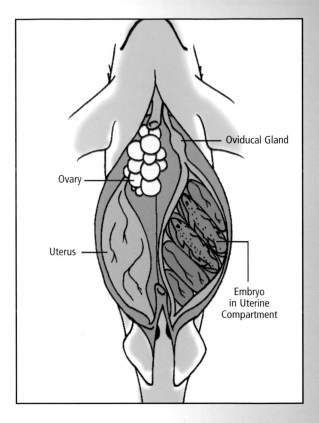

Female shark reproductive system. Illustration by Mike Salavea.

In some sharks, the first few eggs to pass through the oviducal gland are not fertilized but simply act as triggers, readying the gland for active duty. Fertilization, likewise, appears to be a trigger, stimulating production of the egg's protective shell—either a solid, heavy-duty casing in more primitive species such as the whale shark, or a transparent cellophane-like membrane in the blue shark—and preparing the egg for its passage into the uterus. The two hard-working oviducal glands act like production assembly lines, fertilizing and wrapping one egg at a time—up to 300 eggs in the case of the prolific whale shark.

All available data for rays in Hawai'i shows that they bear one-to-seven live pups, which, in the eagle, manta and devil rays are curled—with wings folded around their bodies—in the uterus. These embryonic rays feed on a small egg yolk at first and then receive uterine milk delivered via one-inch-long, finger-like uterine projections called villi (trophonemata). Researchers speculate that this milk allows the pups to grow larger and thus have a better chance of survival.

A mobula (spinetail devil) ray's unborn embryo with wings wrapped around its body (preserved, BPBM).

Sandra Raredon, Smithsonian Institution, NMNH

Life in the Womb

Not all sharks carry their young to term in the same fashion. More primitive sharks such as Hawai'i's spongehead cat shark are oviparous (ovi = egg). They actually lay eggs, attaching them to coral, rocks and any number of handy hitching posts. Pelagic sharks in the open ocean, having no suitable objects for egg anchors, do not lay eggs. Instead, they are viviparous—they bear live young who must immediately fend for themselves with no parental help. These embryonic pups receive nourishment and grow in the womb.

There are four types of live-bearing uterine embryo-development strategies: First, aplacental with one egg—in which the embryo is not attached by any type of placental cord to the uterus and feeds on its own egg yolk; second, aplacental with uterine milk (rays only)—no placental attachment, each embryo uses up its own yolk and then receives milk from uterine villi; third, aplacental oophagous—no placental attachment and embryonic pups eat multiple eggs; and fourth, placental—embryos are attached to the uterus by a placenta.

Larry Ellis

Top: Eggcase from a spongehead cat shark— Hawai'i's only egg-laying shark (preserved).

Bottom: Two piked dogfish (Squalus acanthias) (not in Hawai'i) embryos and their egg yolks.

A Good Egg
(aplacental with one egg)

In the first aplacental group, each embryo feeds on its own egg yolk inside the egg case and is connected to the egg via a stalk. During development, the uterine lining stretches to accommodate the growth of embryos—up to 114 in the prickly shark's case. Little is known about the internal uterine environment surrounding shark egg cases. But we do know that in certain species such as the shortspine spurdog, the uterus flushes with seawater during late pregnancy.

The tiger shark also falls into this aplacental group although its egg wrapping is a transparent membrane rather than a sturdy egg case. Because the female tiger shark can house up to 41 pups in each uterus, and each pup is 30 to 34 inches long just before birth, researchers speculate that the initial egg yolk does not contain enough nourishment to sustain such large-scale growth. Therefore, the embryo must be receiving additional nutrients from the mother via the clear fluid within the membrane, which also acts as a conduit for wastes. In other words, the egg sac together with the fluid surrounding the embryo act much like a traditional placenta. In addition, each tiger shark egg sac rests in its own flexible compartment within the uterus. Because these compartments allow nutrient and gas transfer from fluids in the uterus to the embryo, they also act like placenta. In fact, researchers consider the compartment to be the ancestor of the placenta.

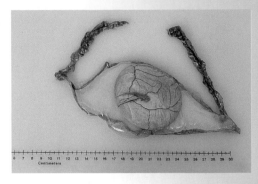

Courtesy of the Waikiki Aquarium.

Top: A tiger shark embryo and yolk inside its transparent egg wrapping.

Center: A stalk connects this tiger shark embryo with its egg yolk.

Below: This brown stingray embryo had almost used up its yolk sac (preserved, BPBM).

(aplacental with uterine milk)

The spotted eagle ray falls into the one-egg-only category, but also bathes each fetus in uterine milk during the later stages of its 11-to-12-month gestation period. Litters of one to four pups, each having a wingspan of 20 to 30 inches and looking like miniature adults, are born in winter. Both spotted eagle and devil rays have been seen dropping their pups while jumping out of the water during the birthing process.

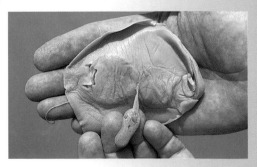

Two embryos in a crocodile shark uterus face towards an approaching torpedo-shaped, nutritive egg.

A supply of eggs (bottom) provides food for growing crocodile shark embryos.

These embryos appear to be about one-third of the way through gestation. Crocodile shark pups are about 16-inches long at birth.

Feasting on Eggs
(aplacental oophagous)

Sharks in the third group also lack a placental attachment to the uterus, but as embryos use up their initial yolk sac, they receive an ample supply of fresh, nutritive eggs from the ovary. Getting out of their egg sacs to eat these nutritive eggs could be a dilemma for young embryonic sharks, but the pelagic thresher, at least, has found a solution. Once the thresher embryos have absorbed the nutrients from their birth egg, they develop tiny teeth, which they use to break through their egg sacs and puncture the sacs of nutritive eggs. As the young sharks grow larger, these embryonic teeth disappear and the newly forming pups swallow nutritive eggs without breaking the sac, digesting the yolk in their swollen bellies over a period of time.

Eating a string of nutrient-laden egg yolks can result in a large embryo. Recent studies by Taiwanese researchers show that egg-eating pelagic thresher sharks, once thought to be 40-inches long at birth, are actually almost six-feet long when born (including their lengthy, whip-like tail). Other sharks that produce nutritive eggs for their young include the crocodile, mako, great white and possibly megamouth, although the latter's uterine development is still unproven.

The sand tiger shark (*Carcharias taurus*) in the Atlantic Ocean practices intra-uterine cannibalism in which the first embryo to develop in each uterus eats its siblings as well as all the nutritive eggs. Are smalltooth and bigeye sand tiger sharks in Hawai'i also uterine cannibals? Researchers speculate that this might be the case.

Attached to Mother
(placental)

Finally, the fourth group of embryos, which includes hammer-head, blue and silky sharks, is nourished via a placenta. As in the first two groups, these embryos feed on their yolk sacs during the first phase of growth. Around the middle of the gestation period, the uterine lining secretes fluids containing nutrients that augment declining yolk stores. Then the yolk sac attaches to the uterine lining becoming a placenta, and nourishment is supplied directly from the mother. In hammerheads, the usually smooth stalk connecting the embryo with its egg yolk sac is encumbered with projections called appendiculae, which may aid nutrient absorption and gas (i.e. oxygen and carbon dioxide) exchange.

Larry Ellis

An embryo attached to its mother's uterine lining.

An umbilical scar shows that this juvenile silky shark was recently attached to its mother by a placenta.

More or Less

The length of time embryos spend in the womb varies widely. The diamond stingray and spotted eagle ray keep their embryonic pups for 11 to 12 months. Blue shark pups emerge in 9 to 12 months, while gestation in frilled sharks may last for 3.5 years. Sharks also disagree on how many pups to produce, with thresher sharks opting for 2-4 young, bluntnose sixgill sharks looking at a possible family of 108, and the whale shark topping out at 300 offspring.

A large number of pups means that each one will be smaller, whereas the same amount of reproductive energy spent producing large pups means they will be fewer in number. There are advantages to both strategies. With a large number of small offspring, chances of at least a few of them surviving are fairly good even under changing and inhospitable environmental conditions. It seems reasonable to expect that larger pups will be stronger and better equipped to survive than their smaller relatives, but if a certain type of shark is plagued by overfishing or other imbalances, fewer pups can lead to a faster species decline. Why a particular shark species has adapted to one or the other strategy still remains a mystery.

Three brown stingray embryos could make up an entire litter (preserved, BPBM).

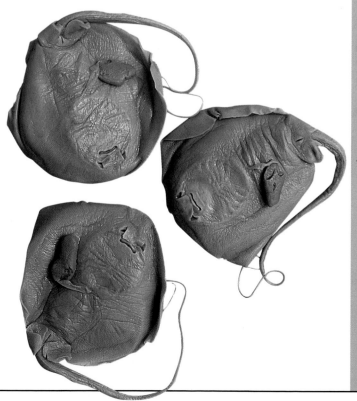

CHAPTER 6

SHARK AND RAY SPECIES:
INTRODUCTION

Details are limited for many of the shark and ray species found in Hawai'i, so even the smallest piece of new information is useful. If you discover any new information, or find any errors in this book, please contact us through the Waikīkī Aquarium so we can keep track of and update the records for Hawai'i's sharks and rays.

On the following pages are descriptions of forty shark and nine ray species found around the Hawaiian Islands. We hope you find this information easy to read and at-your-fingertips accessible, as that was our intent.

The following checklist of species should make locating a particular shark or ray species quick and convenient. Scientific names follow Compagno (1999), except for the diamond stingray, whose scientific name follows Eschmeyer (1998). Throughout this book, when discussing size, we use total lengths for sharks and the torpedo ray (because it has a shark-like tail), and disc width for all other rays. In photographs of sharks and rays stored at the Bernice P. Bishop Museum (BPBM) and the National Museum of Natural History (NMNH), the specimens appear to be a yellowish tan—not their natural color but the result of preservatives. We've noted that fact by including (preserved) in the photo captions.

Although Hawai'i is not its regular habitat, a basking shark was reported in the Islands during an irregular migration. Also, a researcher recorded the tope shark as a Hawai'i resident, but we disagree with this finding. A short account of both sharks appears in this chapter.

Face to face with an oceanic whitetip shark.

For the most part, U.S. measurements have been used throughout this book, but for general reference purposes, you might find these conversion equivalents useful:

1 inch	=	2.54 centimeters
3.281 feet	=	1 meter
39.37 inches	=	1 meter
1 fathom	=	6 feet
1 mile	=	1.61 kilometers
2.205 pounds	=	1 kilogram
1.102 tons	=	1 metric ton (MT)
°Fahrenheit	=	°Celsius multiplied by 1.8, add 32
		°F = (°C x 1.8) + 32
°Celsius	=	0.556 multiplied by the result of °Fahrenheit minus 32
		°C = 0.556 x (°F - 32)

Checklist
Sharks and Rays of Hawai'i
(Scientific names follow Compagno 1999 and Eschmeyer 1998)

Photo: Cynthia Vanderlip

SHARKS
OF HAWAI'I

Whale sharks are gentle giants.

Frilled Shark
Chlamydoselachus anguineus
(OTHER NAMES: Requin lezard, Tiburon anguila)

(preserved, BPBM)

SIZE: Birth size 1.8 ft.; maximum length 6.4 ft.

REPRODUCTION: Live birth, aplacental with one egg: embryos develop in the uterus with no attachment to the uterine lining, but the embryos might receive nutritional secretions from the mother. Both ovaries are functional, but only the right uterus is used. There is no clear-cut reproductive season—pups are born throughout the year—and gestation might last for 3.5 years. Litter size ranges from 2-10 pups. Males mature at about 3.2 ft., females mature at about 4.6 ft.

(preserved, BPBM)

HABITAT: A pelagic shark found in all oceans from 65 to 4,200 feet. Hawaiian records show the frilled shark caught over Colahan Seamount by trawl at about 820 feet.

DESCRIPTION: Color: brown. A rare, eel-like shark with a flexible body, six frilled gill slits and distinctive tricuspid teeth.

BIOLOGY: The frilled shark eats both bottom-dwelling and pelagic squid (60.5% of its diet) and fish (10.5%).

NOTES: Danger Rating: Minimal, due to its deep-water habitat, but can be dangerous if handled.

ORDER/FAMILY: Hexanchiformes/Chlamydoselachidae

REFERENCES: Compagno, 1984; Borets, 1986; Tanaka et al., 1990; Kubota et al., 1991.

Bluntnose Sixgill Shark
Hexanchus griseus
(OTHER NAMES: Requin griset)

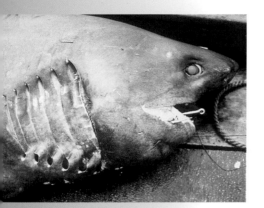

SIZE: Birth size 25-28 in.; maximum length 16 ft.

REPRODUCTION: Live birth, aplacental with one egg: embryos develop in the uterus with no attachment to the uterine lining. Litters range from 22-108 pups. Males mature at about 9.5 ft, females mature at about 13.5 ft.

HABITAT: A coastal and deep-water shark found in temperate and tropical regions of all oceans and the Mediterranean Sea from the surface to 8,200 feet. Hawaiian records indicate it is caught at depths of 360 to 4,724 feet at temperatures from 39°F to 53.5°F throughout the main and Northwestern Hawaiian Islands.

Gordon Hubbell

Upper jaw teeth.

Gordon Hubbell

Lower jaw teeth.

DESCRIPTION: Color: darkish brown. A large shark with a broadly rounded snout, six gill slits, one dorsal fin, small green eyes with no nictitating membrane, and distinctive comb-like teeth in its lower jaw.

BIOLOGY: When captured on longline hooks, this shark is sluggish and appears sensitive to bright light. It feeds on a wide variety of prey including shrimp, crab, squid, octopus, other sharks, bony fish and marine mammals. Because it is captured near the surface as well as at great depths, researchers speculate that the bluntnose sixgill scavenges food from the sea floor and also uses a vertical migration feeding strategy. Fossils of this primitive shark have been discovered from the Cretaceous and Tertiary periods.

NOTES: Danger Rating: Minimal, due to its mostly deep-water habitat.

ORDER/FAMILY: Hexanchiformes/Hexanchidae

REFERENCES: Compagno, 1984; Chave and Jones, 1991; Crow et al., 1996.

Prickly Shark
Echinorhinus cookei

(OTHER NAMES: Squalae boucie du Pacifique,
Tiburon negro espinoso, Cooke's shark)

Photo courtesy of Andrew Stewart,
Museum of New Zealand.

SIZE: Birth size 15-18 in.;
maximum length 13 ft.

REPRODUCTION: Assumed aplacental with
one egg, but little is known. A pregnant
female captured in Hawai'i contained
114 pups averaging 9.5 inches in length.
It appears that each embryo feeds on its
own yolk sac and is born live. Males mature
at 6 ft., females mature at 6.5 ft.

Courtesy of HURL

HABITAT: A normally deep- and cold-water
shark found only in the Pacific Ocean at
depths of 36 to 1,651 feet. Hawaiian depth
records range from 580 to 1,378 feet.
Submersible observers report the prickly shark
swimming slowly near the ocean floor.

DESCRIPTION: Color: grayish brown
with black distal margins (outer edges of
fins). Two dorsal fins (the first is posterior
to the origin of the pelvic fin), no anal fin,
and protruding thorn-like scales.

Gordon Hubbell

Teeth of a 6'8" prickly shark.

BIOLOGY: A fisherman caught the first known prickly shark in
1928 off Kaua'i and took it to the Honolulu fish market for sale.
Its diet consists of squid, octopus, other sharks and bony fish.

NOTES: Danger Rating: None, due to its deep-water habitat.

ORDER/FAMILY: Squaliformes/Echinorhinidae

REFERENCES: Compagno, 1984; Chave and Mundy, 1994;
Crow et al., 1996.

Shortspine Spurdog Shark
Squalus mitsukurii
(OTHER NAMES: greeneye spurdog, aliguillat epinette, galludo espinilla)

SIZE: Birth size 8.6-11 in.; maximum length 3.6 ft.

REPRODUCTION: Live birth, aplacental with one egg: Embryos feed on yolk reserves only, develop in packets in the uterus, and are not attached to the uterine lining. Litters range from 1-6 pups. Thought to be a slow-growing species, males mature at 16-19 in. in 14 years, and females at 25-27 in. in 15 years.

HABITAT: A deep-water shark seen resting on the sea floor and swimming just above it in the Pacific, Atlantic and Indian Oceans, often near seamounts. Water temperature influences this shark's depth range, and it has been captured in 13 feet of cold water off the coast of New Zealand and from 300 to 2,424 feet in the Northwestern Hawaiian Islands.

DESCRIPTION: Color: gray. A small shark with green eyes, a prominent spine in front of both dorsal fins, and no anal fin.

BIOLOGY: The shortspine spurdog might live more than 27 years. Late female maturity puts this shark at risk from overfishing, especially around seamounts where fishing fleets know they can find it in abundance. Food consists primarily of crustaceans, squid, octopus and bony fish. A National Marine Fisheries Service survey revealed that heavy fishing of this shark at Hancock Seamount resulted in a 50% decline in the species (as measured by the catch rate) between 1985 and 1988.

NOTES: Danger Rating: None in Hawai'i due to its deep-sea habitat and small size.

ORDER/FAMILY: Squaliformes/Squalidae

REFERENCES: Compagno, 1984; Chave and Mundy, 1994; Wilson and Seki, 1994.

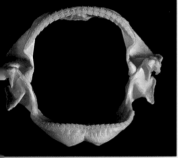

Above: Jaw with teeth; lower jaw cutting teeth.

Below: Swimming near the deep-ocean floor.

Photo courtesy of HURL.

Mosaic Gulper Shark
Centrophorus tesselatus
(OTHER NAMES: Squale-chagrin mosaique, Quelvacho mosaico)

Courtesy of HURL.

SIZE: Birth size unknown, only a few specimens have been found; maximum length 2.9 ft. In Hawai'i, size range is 2.1-2.9 ft.

REPRODUCTION: Live birth, aplacental with one egg; It is thought that embryos develop in the uterus with no attachment to the uterine lining, and each embryo receives nourishment from its individual yolk sac only.

HABITAT: A deep-water shark found near the ocean floor off Japan and Hawai'i (see **Notes** below). This shark has been captured at depths of 853 to 2,390 feet. In Hawai'i, it has been captured in gill nets or observed at 853 to 1,640 feet.

DESCRIPTION: **Color:** light grayish brown with green eyes. No anal fin, and well-developed dorsal fin spines.

BIOLOGY: No data available.

NOTES: **Danger Rating:** None, due to its small size and deep-water habitat. This shark is very similar to the gulper shark *(Centrophorus granulosus)*, which has recently been noted as present in Hawai'i (Chave and Malahoff, 1998). However, are both species present in Hawai'i or just one? A thorough revision of the genus *Centrophorus* is in order.

ORDER/FAMILY: Squaliformes/Centrophoridae

REFERENCES: Clarke, 1972; Compagno, 1984; Chave and Malahoff, 1998.

Combtooth Dogfish
Centroscyllium nigrum
(OTHER NAMES: Aiguillat peigne, Tollo negro peine)

Leonard Compagno

SIZE: Birth size is unknown; maximum length 1.6 ft. Size range at capture: 13.8-19.7 in.

REPRODUCTION: Presumed live birth, aplacental with one egg; each embryo receives nourishment from its individual yolk sac only with no attachment to the uterine lining. Males mature at 14 in.; female maturity size is unknown.

HABITAT: A bottom-dwelling shark found only in the Pacific Ocean off Hawai'i, Southern California, Panama, Cocos Island, Galapagos Islands and South America. In most areas, this shark has been captured at depths of 720 to 3,750 feet. In Hawai'i, it has been caught in trawls along the bottom at 2,500 to 3,000 feet.

DESCRIPTION: Color: black with white-tipped pectoral, pelvic and dorsal fins; well-developed dorsal spines; no anal fin; and teeth that resemble a comb.

BIOLOGY: Diet is unknown.

NOTES: Danger Rating: None, due to its deep-water habitat and small size. **Outdated Scientific Names**: *Centroscyllium ruscosum*

ORDER/FAMILY: Squaliformes/Etmopteridae

REFERENCES: Gilbert, 1905; Clarke, 1972; Compagno, 1984.

Blurred Smooth Lantern Shark

Etmopterus bigelowi

(OTHER NAMES: none)

SIZE: Birth size is unknown; maximum length 2.2 ft.

REPRODUCTION: Live birth, aplacental with one egg: little is known; presumably embryos develop in the uterus with no attachment to the uterine lining. Males mature at about 1.4 ft., females mature at about 1.6 ft.

HABITAT: Found in all oceans at depths of 534 to 3,300 feet. In Hawai'i, two bottom longline records show that this shark has been caught over the Hancock (at about 1,300 feet) and Pensacola Seamounts.

DESCRIPTION: Color: black. A small shark with dorsal-fin spines and no anal fin. Scales are not arranged in a pattern. This species was originally confused with the smooth lantern shark.

BIOLOGY: Examined stomach contents included squid and bony fish.

NOTES: Danger Rating: None, due to size and deep-water habitat.

ORDER/FAMILY: Squaliformes/Etmopteridae

REFERENCES: Shirai and Tachikawa, 1993.

Teeth, male.

Teeth, female.

Blackbelly Lantern Shark
Etmopterus lucifer
(OTHER NAMES: Sagre lucifer, Tollo lucero diablo, Lucifer shark)

Teeth, male.

SIZE: Birth size is less than 6 in.; maximum length 1 ft. 7 in.

REPRODUCTION: Live birth, aplacental with one egg: embryos develop in the uterus with no attachment to the uterine lining, and each embryo receives nourishment from its individual yolk sac only. Six to 8 eggs were found in one uterus. Males mature at 7 in., females mature at 8 in.

HABITAT: A deep-water shark found in all oceans near the sea floor and at depths of 600 to 6,560 feet. In the Northwestern Hawaiian Islands, it has been caught in trawls at 885 to 1,300 feet.

DESCRIPTION: Color: a light brown back merging into darker brown sides. Scales are arranged in rows, and no anal fin.

BIOLOGY: Vertical migrator. Diet consists of squid, bony fish (primarily lantern fish) and crustaceans.

NOTES: Danger Rating: None, due to its deep-water habitat.

ORDER/FAMILY: Squaliformes/Etmopteridae

REFERENCES: Myagkov and Kondyurin, 1976; Compagno, 1984; Borets, 1986.

Smooth Lantern Shark
Etmopterus pusillus
(OTHER NAMES: Sagre nain, Tollo lucero liso)

SIZE: Birth size is unknown; maximum length 1.6 ft.

REPRODUCTION: Live birth, aplacental with one egg: Little is known; presumably embryos develop in the uterus with no attachment to the uterine lining. Both males and females mature at about 1.2 ft.

HABITAT: A pelagic shark found in all oceans at depths of 900 to 3,400 feet and occasionally at the surface over deep-water. In Hawai'i, it has been caught over the Hancock Seamount.

DESCRIPTION: Color: black. A small shark with dorsal-fin spines and no anal fin. Scales are not arranged in a pattern. The smooth lantern shark is often confused with the blurred smooth lantern shark.

BIOLOGY: Diet consists of squid, small sharks and bony fish.

NOTES: Danger Rating: None, due to small size and deep-water habitat.

ORDER/FAMILY: Squaliformes/Etmopteridae

REFERENCES: Compagno, 1984; Shirai and Tachikawa, 1993.

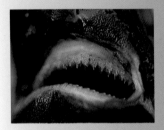

Teeth, male.

Hawaiian Lantern Shark
Etmopterus villosus
(OTHER NAMES: Sagre diablotin, Tollo lucero de Hawai'i)

Sandra Raredon, Smithsonian Institution, NMNH (preserved)

SIZE: Birth size unknown. Only a few specimens have been caught. Size ranges from 5-18 in.

REPRODUCTION: Live birth, aplacental with one egg: Little is known; presumably embryos develop in the uterus with no attachment to the uterine lining.

HABITAT: The original specimen was captured off the south coast of Moloka'i in 1902 at a depth somewhere between 1,300 and 3,000 feet. Reported seen from a submersible off the Big Island of Hawai'i, but this observation cannot be verified.

DESCRIPTION: Color: black. A small shark with spines on the dorsal fins, no anal fin, and scales that are lined up in rows, particularly from the second dorsal fin to the tail.

BIOLOGY: Nothing is known about diet.

NOTES: Danger Rating: None, due to size and deep-water habitat.

ORDER/FAMILY: Squaliformes/Etmopteridae

REFERENCES: Gilbert, 1905; Compagno, 1984; Chave and Jones, 1991.

Sandra Raredon, Smithsonian Institution, NMNH (preserved)

Scales line up in rows.

Sandra Raredon, Smithsonian Institution, NMNH (preserved)

Viper Dogfish
Trigonognathus kabeyai
(OTHER NAMES: viper shark)

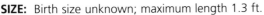

SIZE: Birth size unknown; maximum length 1.3 ft.

REPRODUCTION: Live birth, aplacental with one egg: presumably embryos develop in the uterus with no attachment to the uterine lining. Males mature at 14 in.

HABITAT: A pelagic shark and newly described species. Caught in Japan at 1,100 feet; caught in Hawai'i over Hancock Seamount at 885 feet.

DESCRIPTION: Color: brownish-black. A small shark with dorsal-fin spines, no anal fin, and fang-like teeth.

BIOLOGY: Diet consists of crustaceans and bony fish.

NOTES: Danger Rating: Minimal, due to size and deep-water habitat.

ORDER/FAMILY: Sqaualiformes/Etmopteridae

REFERENCES: Mochizuki and Ohe, 1990; Wetherbee and Kajiura, 2000.

Velvet Dogfish
Scymnodon squamulosus
(OTHER NAMES: Squale-grogneur veloute,
Bruga boccachia, Bruja terciopelo,)

SIZE: Birth size unknown; maximum length 2.8 ft.

REPRODUCTION: Live birth, aplacental with one egg: presumably embryos develop in the uterus with no attachment to the uterine lining. 3-10 eggs have been seen in the ovaries. Males mature at about 1.6 ft., females mature at about 2.5 ft.

HABITAT: A pelagic shark found in all oceans from the surface to 6,500 feet. Hawaiian records show the velvet dogfish caught north of Kaua'i at about 98 feet.

DESCRIPTION: Color: black. A relatively small shark with a flat head; broad, leaf-shaped pectoral fins; spines on dorsal fins; and no anal fin.

BIOLOGY: Diet is unknown.

NOTES: Danger Rating: Minimal, due to offshore and deep-water habitat.

ORDER/FAMILY: Squaliformes/Somnosidae

REFERENCES: Compagno, 1984; Wetherbee and Crow, 1996.

Kitefin Shark
Dalatias licha
(OTHER NAMES: Squale liche, Carocho)

Brad Wetherbee

Gordon Hubbell

Upper jaw teeth.

Gordon Hubbell

Lower jaw teeth.

SIZE: Birth size about 1 ft.; maximum length 5.3 ft.

REPRODUCTION: Live birth, aplacental with one egg: embryos develop in the uterus with no attachment to the uterine lining. Litter size ranges from 10-16 pups. Males mature at about 2.5 ft., females mature at about 3.9 ft.

HABITAT: A pelagic shark found in selective areas of all oceans from 120 to 5,900 feet, and probably more common than currently documented. Hawaiian records show this shark caught by trawl off Maui and Colahan Seamount at about 1,000 feet.

DESCRIPTION: Color: black. A powerful deep-sea shark with a blunt snout; two almost-equal-size dorsal fins with no spines; no anal fin; and triangular, saw-like teeth in the lower jaw.

BIOLOGY: Diet consists of worms, cephalopods, crustaceans, sharks, rays and bony fish.

NOTES: Danger Rating: Minimal, due to its deep-water habitat.

ORDER/FAMILY: Squaliformes/Dalatiidae

REFERENCES: Struhsaker, 1973; Compagno, 1984; Borets, 1986; Last and Stevens, 1994, Compagno and Cook, 1996.

Brad Wetherbee

Pygmy Shark
Euprotomicrus bispinatus
(OTHER NAMES: Squale pygmee, Tollo pigmeo)

SIZE: Birth size about 4 in.; maximum length 11 in.

REPRODUCTION: Live birth, aplacental with one egg. Embryos develop in the uterus with no attachment to the uterine lining. Litters of 8 have been reported. Males mature at about 7 in., femals mature at about 9 in.

HABITAT: A pelagic shark found in all oceans from the surface to at least 1,300 feet. This species appears to be an active vertical migrator. In Hawai'i, it has been spotted at the surface off Kona on the Big Island.

DESCRIPTION: Color: black. The smallest shark, the pygmy has a short first-dorsal fin, no dorsal-fin spines and no anal fin.

BIOLOGY: Diet consists of crustaceans, squid and bony fish.

NOTES: Danger Rating: None, due to its small size and open-ocean habitat.

ORDER/FAMILY: Squaliformes/Dalatiidae

REFERENCES: Compagno, 1984.

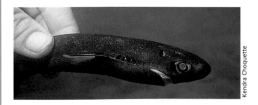

Kendra Choquette

Kendra Choquette

Cookiecutter Shark
Isistius brasiliensis

(OTHER NAMES: tollo cigarro, squalelet feroce, luminous shark, cigar shark)

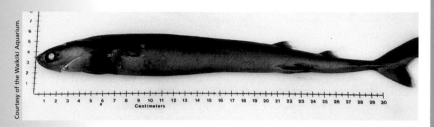

Courtesy of the Waikīkī Aquarium.

Cookiecutter bite mark in a freshly caught tuna.

SIZE: Birth size is unknown, although 9 embryos found in one cookiecutter ranged in size from 4.75-5 in.; maximum length 20 in.

REPRODUCTION: Live birth, aplacental with one egg; each embryo feeds on its own egg with no placental attachment; 6 to 12 large eggs have been found in a cookiecutter uterus. Males mature at 12-15.5 in. and females mature at 15-17 in.

HABITAT: A wide-ranging circumtropical pelagic shark found in the Pacific, Atlantic and Indian oceans, it is caught at night, sometimes at the surface and sometimes at depths up to 11,500 ft.—a remarkable depth range, especially for such a small shark. The cookiecutter is thought to be a vertical migrator, and if its depth range proves accurate, this shark climbs the equivalent of Japan's Mount Fuji every day. Most likely it migrates from the surface down to the thermocline—roughly 330 ft—with occasional forays into deeper water.

DESCRIPTION AND BIOLOGY: Color: brownish black with a dark collar around the gill region and bright green eyes. Known as a parasitic shark, the cookiecutter feeds on plugs of tissue from fish and mammals much larger than itself. It attaches its sucker-type lips, drives razor-sharp, saw-like lower teeth into the skin and flesh of its victim, twists to cut out a conical plug of flesh, then pulls free with the plug held by the hook-like upper teeth. These "crater" wounds—the size of golf balls—are evident on marlin, tuna, swordfish and other large fish at fish auctions and were originally thought to be caused by bacteria or invertebrate parasites until they were connected to the cookiecutter. This little shark also feeds on crustaceans and squid with bodies almost as large as itself and has been known to attack the slow-moving megamouth shark as well as U.S. Navy submarines, leaving its distinctive mark on the rubber sonardomes.

Mouth and teeth. (preserved, BPBM)

79

A bioluminescent area covers the entire lower surface of its trunk with the exception of the fins and dark collar marking. It is thought that the bioluminescence might be used as a lure to attract unsuspecting fish or marine mammals to an easy meal, whereupon the cookiecutter turns the tables and becomes the predator.

The small paired fins, long body cavity and oily liver of this shark suggest that it is neutrally buoyant and not dependent on forward motion and fins for dynamic lift. It also has a more highly calcified, therefore stronger, skeleton than other sharks of its type—probably a necessary adaptation for gouging the flesh of larger animals. It can be quick and active when caught and can bite its captors if they are not careful. Rarely seen swimming in its natural environment, it has been reported glowing a bright green.

NOTES: Danger Rating: Minimal. Because this shark is not found in nearshore coastal areas, the chance of a swimmer or diver being attacked is remote, though possible. On July 23, 1992, a fisherman named Zosimo Popa was found drowned 15 miles off the coast of Wai'anae. Although tied to a floating ice chest, he had two cookiecutter bites in his lower back that were probably post-mortem. **Economic Impact:** Cookiecutter bites damage the flesh of market fish.

ORDER/FAMILY: Squaliformes/Dalatiidae

REFERENCES: Jones 1971; Compagno 1984; Amorim et al, 1998.

Whale Shark
Rhincodon typus
(OTHER NAMES: Requin baline, Tiburon ballena)

SIZE: Birth size 21.5 - 26 in.; maximum length 45 ft. One 27-year-old female was measured at 31.5 ft.

REPRODUCTION: Live birth, aplacental with one egg: the whale shark is a transition species between egg-laying and live bearing; pups inside egg cases hatch in the uterus as opposed to outside the mother as with other egg-case-producing sharks. Egg cases are 8.3 in. long and 8 in. wide—a tight fit for the 21-26 in. pup. They also lack the tendrils and are not as tough as the "mermaid's purses" deposited on seaweed or rocks by many egg-laying sharks. One female contained 300 egg cases. After birth, small whale shark pups are usually found between the equator and about 20° north latitude in the North Pacific Ocean. Females are immature up to 18 ft., and one mature female was measured at 35 ft.; males mature at 28.2 ft. and 20 years old.

HABITAT: A pelagic shark found in all oceans and the Red Sea, whale sharks are often observed feeding at the surface. Kukuyev (1996) reports very young (birth to two years old) whale sharks caught at 8,500 to 15,000 feet in both the Atlantic and Pacific oceans. In Hawai'i, they are rarely found north of Kaua'i.

DESCRIPTION: The whale shark is the largest fish in the ocean. It has a nearly terminal mouth, 300 rows of backcurved teeth, which are not used in feeding, and a unique checkerboard spot pattern on its body.

BIOLOGY: A filter feeder (see **Chapter 4: Feeding Habits**), the whale shark is often seen with its mouth open, feeding on swarms of zooplankton (copepods, krill) squid and fish, sometimes swimming vertically, straight up towards the surface, and at other times swimming normally (its cruising speed is 2 mph). When feeding in a vertical position the whale shark often breaks the surface, then pushes itself up and down with its tail, catching fish that sometimes jump into its open mouth. In Hawai'i, the whale shark is usually seen alone. However, during coral spawning periods in Australia when coral reproductive eggs and sperm are released into the water en masse, these sharks tend to congregate (up to 4 sharks per 6/10 of a mile) to feed on massive swarms of zooplankton, which have gathered to feast on the coral eggs.

NOTES: Danger Rating: Minimal because the whale shark is a filter feeder. But because of their size, whale sharks have caused damage to boats and bumped into unwary snorkelers and divers. **Economic Impact:** Whale shark watching is a potential source of ecotourism dollars. Also, in India, Taiwan and the Philippines, the whale shark is part of a seasonal fishery.

The meat is salted and used as a staple food in many villages, made into sashimi, or served wok-fried with scallions, ginger and saki. In 1995 in Taiwan, whale shark meat cost 400 N.T.D. (New Taiwanese Dollars) per kilogram, the highest price paid for commercial shark meat. As many as 100 whale sharks per year are reported killed by Taiwanese fishermen using harpoons, and there is some indication that the whale shark population might have declined in recent years. Whale shark fins are marketed for shark-fin soup, and the jaws are also sold.

ORDER/FAMILY: Orectolobiformes/Rhincodontidae

REFERENCES: Compagno, 1984; Joung et al., 1996; Kukuyev, 1996; Taylor, 1996; Clark and Nelson, 1997; Winter, 2000; Eckert and Stewart, 2001.

Smalltooth Sand Tiger Shark
Odontaspis ferox
(OTHER NAMES: Requin feroce, Solrayo)

(preserved, BPBM)

SIZE: Birth size estimated at 3 ft.; maximum length 12 ft.

REPRODUCTION: Very little is known. Intra-uterine cannibalism (in each uterus, one embryo eats the other embryos and eggs) is possible. Males mature at about 9 ft., female maturity size is not known.

HABITAT: A pelagic shark found in all oceans and the Mediterranean Sea from 42 to 2,700 feet. Only a few specimens have been seen at scattered locations worldwide. Hawaiian records show that three smalltooth sand tigers were caught— two in a gill net at 600-1,000 feet off Barbers Point, O'ahu; and the other on a longline at 800 feet off Lisianski Atoll in the Northwestern Hawaiian Islands.

DESCRIPTION: Color: medium gray, sometimes with scattered, darker-reddish spots. A large, bulky shark with a pointed snout and two large dorsal fins. Each tooth generally sports 2-3 pairs of cusps.

BIOLOGY: Diet consists of crustaceans, squid, rays and bony fish.

NOTES: Danger Rating: Minimal, due to its deep-water habitat.

ORDER/FAMILY: Lamniformes/Odontaspididae

REFERENCES: Clarke, 1972; Compagno, 1984; Seigel and Compagno, 1986; Yano and Kugai, 1993.

Bigeye Sand Tiger Shark
Odontaspis noronhai
(OTHER NAMES: Requin noronhai, Solrayo ojigrande)

Bob Humphreys

SIZE: Birth size is unknown; largest speciman measured 11.5 ft.

REPRODUCTION: Very little is known. Intra-uterine cannibalism (in each uterus, one embryo eats the other embryos and eggs) is possible. Males mature at about 10.6 ft., females mature at about 10.7 ft.

HABITAT: A pelagic shark found in all oceans from 328 to 3,300 feet. Only a few specimens have been caught at scattered locations. Hawaiian records from southwest of the Big Island report finding this shark at a depth of 1,500 feet.

DESCRIPTION: Color: uniform dark chocolate brown. This shark has a pointed snout, two large dorsal fins, and two cusps per tooth, one on either side.

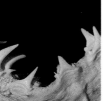
Gordon Hubbell

BIOLOGY: Examined stomach contents included bony fish, although little is known about dietary habits.

NOTES: Danger Rating: Minimal, due to deep-water habitat.

ORDER/FAMILY: Lamniformes/Odontaspididae

REFERENCES: Compagno, 1984; Humphreys et al. 1989.

Bob Humphreys

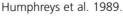

Bob Humphreys

Crocodile Shark
Pseudocarcharias kamoharai
(OTHER NAMES: Requin crocodile, Tiburon cocodrilo)

SIZE: Birth size about 16 in.; maximum length 3.6 ft.

REPRODUCTION: Live birth, aplacental oophagous: no uterine attachment; embryos are supplied with multiple ovarian eggs in the uterus. Normal litter size: 4, two embryos in each uterus. Embryos face toward the oviduct in middle gestation to swallow eggs as they enter the uterus. Males mature at 2.4 ft., females mature at 2.9 ft.

HABITAT: A pelagic shark found in all oceans from the surface to about 1,900 feet.

DESCRIPTION: Color: dark brown. A slender shark with large eyes, pointed snout, large gill slits, well-developed tail, a large liver rich in squaline, and spike teeth.

BIOLOGY: The crocodile shark has powerful jaws and jaw muscles, snaps forcefully and vigorously when captured, and can protrude its mouth a considerable distance from its head. Feeds on crustaceans, cephalopods such as shrimp and squid, and bony fish.

NOTES: Danger Rating: Minimal due to its offshore and deep-water habitat.

ORDER/FAMILY: Lamniformes/Pseudocarchariidae

REFERENCES: Compagno, 1984; Last and Stevens, 1994.

Crocodile shark embryos.

Megamouth Shark
Megachasma pelagios
(OTHER NAMES: Tiburon bacudo, requin grande gueule)

SIZE: Birth size unknown; maximum length known: 17 ft..

REPRODUCTION: Presumed aplacental oophagous, although no embryos have been seen yet. Megamouth is presumed to bear live young, and embryos may receive nutrition from oophagy (egg eating) like most lamnid sharks. Little is known about size at maturity, but according to the size of her reproductive organs, a 15-foot female had not yet arrived at maturity. However, a 14.6-foot male weighing 1,653 pounds was found to be mature.

HABITAT: A wide-ranging pelagic shark, the megamouth has been found in the Pacific, Atlantic and Indian Oceans. An acoustically tracked megamouth showed vertical movements, swimming in shallow waters 40 to 82 feet deep at night and descending to depths of 394 to 634 feet during the day, with the steepest ascent and descent occurring at dusk and dawn.

The megamouth—a very large, bizarre, filter-feeding shark—was first captured in 1976 near Hawai'i. Since then, 14 additional megamouths have been caught. One was caught, tagged and released; another was caught and released without being tagged; but none have been seen swimming freely. However, ten days before the sixth megamouth was caught off the coast of California in 1990, an unidentified large black fish was seen swimming in the area. It did not have the arched back of a diving marine mammal and did not blow a water spout—typical whale behavior. Could it have been megamouth? The Hawaiian megamouth—caught when its mouth and teeth became entangled in a pair of parachutes used by a U.S. Navy research vessel as drifting boat anchors—is preserved at the Bernice P. Bishop Museum in Honolulu. Other specimens are on display at the Los Angeles Natural History Museum and Marine World umino-nakamichi in Fukuoka, Japan. A non-displayed specimen is stored at the Western Australian Museum in Perth.

DESCRIPTION: Short, broadly-rounded snout; very large and long head; huge mouth that extends behind the eyes when fully open; large upper lobe of tail much longer than lower lobe; white-tipped pectoral fins; eyes without nictitating eyelids; teeth greatly reduced; soft fins; contains less calcium in its cartilaginous skeleton than do other filter-feeding sharks such as the basking and whale sharks, suggesting that it is less active. That fact, plus a large liver that contains abundant low-density oil, along with its flabby body, may help the megamouth to maintain near-neutral buoyancy. The internal gill arches are lined with dense rows of papillose gill rakers that trap food and prevent it from being expelled through the gills. Silvery, luminescent tissue lines the inside of the mouth.

BIOLOGY: Swimming speed is thought to be 0.9 to 1.3 miles per hour. In 1961, 26-million-year-old shark fossil teeth were discovered in an early Miocene sand deposit, the Jewett Sand, in Kern County, California. Scientists did not know at the time what type of shark teeth they were looking at, but after the first living megamouth was found and examined, researchers were able to identify the fossil teeth as being of similar type and from a close relative of the megamouth. The feeding behavior of megamouth is unlike that of other filter-feeding sharks such as the basking shark, which simply collects food in its wide open mouth. In contrast, megamouth can suddenly open and protrude its jaws to create a vacuum-like suction within its mouth, instantly inhaling food like an underwater slurp gun. Megamouth is a zooplankton filter feeder with stomach contents that include shrimp, copepods and jellyfish. Shrimp and other small prey might also be drawn to the silvery mouth lining.

NOTES: Danger Rating: Minimal because megamouth is a deep-water, filter-feeding shark.

ORDER/FAMILY: Lamniformes/Megachasmidae

REFERENCES: Taylor et al., 1983; Compagno, 1990; Lavenberg, 1991; Yano et al., 1997; Nelson et al., 1997; Amorium et al., 1998; 2000.

Pelagic Thresher Shark
Alopias pelagicus

(OTHER NAMES: Renard pelagique, Zorro pelagico;
Hawaiian: manō hi'ukā, manō laukāhi'u)

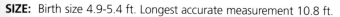

SIZE: Birth size 4.9-5.4 ft. Longest accurate measurement 10.8 ft.

REPRODUCTION: Live birth, aplacental oophagous: Embryo uses up initial yolk sac in uterus, then receives torpedo-shaped eggs for food. Normal litter size: 2, with one in each uterus. Mating and pupping occur throughout the year. Gestation period is unknown. Years to reproductive maturity: Female estimated at 8-9 years; male estimated at 7-8 years. Males mature at 8.7-9 ft, females mature at 9.2-9.6 ft.

HABITAT: A pelagic shark found in the Pacific and Indian Oceans and the Red Sea. Since 1901 in Hawaiian waters, the pelagic thresher has been confused with the common thresher shark—which is not found near Hawai'i. Worldwide, pelagic threshers have been captured from the surface to 500 ft., and one thresher shark sighting by a submersible at 1,200 ft. has not been verified as a pelagic thresher.

DESCRIPTION: Color: bluish/black; white abdomen marking does not extend above pectoral fin bases (insertion). Tail's upper caudal lobe is nearly as long as the shark's body.

BIOLOGY: Examined stomach contents usually consist of squid and bony fish. The long tail is used like a whip to herd fish into a concentrated school or to stun prey. As a result, the pelagic thresher is frequently caught by its tail in fishery longlines.

NOTES: Danger Rating: Minimal, due to its offshore habitat. **Economic Impact:** Along with mako sharks, threshers are regularly sold at the fish auction in Honolulu.

ORDER/FAMILY: Lamniformes/Alopiidae

REFERENCES: Compagno, 1984, Liu et al., 1999; Chave and Malahoff, 1998; Crow et al., in preparation.

Bigeye Thresher Shark
Alopias superciliosus

(OTHER NAMES: Renard a gros yeux, Zorro ojon;
Hawaiian: manō hi'ukā, manō laukāhi'u)

SIZE: Birth size 4.2 ft.
Maximum length 14.8 ft.

REPRODUCTION: Live birth, aplacental
oophagous: Embryo uses up initial yolk sac
in uterus, then receives torpedo-shaped eggs for
food. Normal litter size: 2, with one in each uterus.
Mating and pupping occur throughout the year.
Gestation period is unknown. Years to reproductive
maturity: female estimated at 12-13 years; male
estimated at 9-10 years. Males mature at 8.8-9.4 ft,
females mature at 10.9-11.2 ft.

HABITAT: Found in all oceans and the Mediterranean Sea
from the surface to at least 1,600 feet. In Hawai'i, this shark
is generally caught on fishing lines below 650 feet, and an
increase in bigeye tuna fishing has resulted in more bigeye
thresher shark captures.

DESCRIPTION: Color: dark brown. Tail's upper caudal lobe is
nearly as long as the shark's body. Noticeable by a distinctive,
V-shaped notch on top of the head, and large eyes that can
see objects above as well as to the side.

BIOLOGY: Diet consists of squid and bony fish.
The long tail is used like a whip to herd fish into
a concentrated school or to stun prey. As a result,
the bigeye thresher is frequently caught by its tail
on fishery longlines.

NOTES: Danger Rating: Minimal, due to offshore
and depth habitat. **Economic Impact:** Thresher sharks
are sold at Honolulu's fish auction along with makos.

ORDER/FAMILY: Lamniformes/Alopiidae

REFERENCES: Compagno, 1984; Chen et al., 1997;
Liu et al., 1998; Crow et al., in preparation.

*A bigeye thresher shark is
recognizable by its distinctive
V-shaped head groove.*

*The bullet-shaped head
and upward-seeing eyes
of the bigeye thresher.*

Great White Shark
Carcharodon carcharias

(OTHER NAMES: white pointer, white death, Grand requin blanc, Jaqueton blanco; **Hawaiian:** niuhi)

Ian Gordon

SIZE: Birth size 3.9-4.9 ft.; maximum length 21 ft. The largest male reliably measured was 18 ft. No juvenile great white sharks have been caught in Hawai'i; males and females in Hawai'i have ranged in length from 10 ft. 10 in. to 13 ft. 4 in.

REPRODUCTION: Live birth, aplacental oophagous: no uterine attachment; embryo feeds on its own egg yolk, then receives extra eggs during development. Litter size ranges from 2-14 pups. Pregnant females are rarely seen. Males mature at 11.8 ft., females mature at 14.8-16 ft., reaching a much larger size than males. Researchers studying South African great whites estimated that males reach maturity at 8-10 years and females at 10-12 years.

HABITAT: A coastal and pelagic shark inhabiting continental and island shelves in all temperate to tropical oceans and the Mediterranean Sea from the surface to 4,000 feet. Hawaiian records show that this shark has been caught off O'ahu, Maui and the Big Island at depths from 30 to 156 feet. No great white sharks have ever been caught in the Northwestern Hawaiian Islands.

Great whites, it seems, have a secret life at sea. Often observed around islands and near the coasts of continents, great whites can also travel across vast stretches of open ocean according to a recent study. Of the six sharks fitted with pop-up satellite tags (see **Chapter 7: Science and Sharks**) at seal rookeries off the coast of California, one (a 14-foot male, named Tipfin by the researchers) migrated 2,280 miles to the uninhabited Hawaiian island of Kaho'olawe and stayed there for about four months between December 2000 and April 2001. During his journey, Tipfin traveled at a rate of 43 miles a day and, along with three other long-distance-traveling great whites in the study, spent 90% of his time at two depth ranges: within 15 feet of the surface in colder waters, and between 900 and 1,500 feet below sea level in more tropical climes. Were the sharks following a primal migratory route, searching for different prey, or heading for a mating rendezvous? The answer to that question is still a mystery.

DESCRIPTION: Color: gray with white underside. A large shark with a conical snout, large gill slits, sharp triangular teeth, a strong keel, and a nearly symmetrical tail.

BIOLOGY: This shark is capable of sudden high-speed dashes and sometimes jumps completely out of the water. During elephant seal pupping season at the Farallon Islands off California, larger great whites (14-16 feet) appeared to take up residence and patrol more limited home ranges than slightly smaller (12-13 feet) great whites. We can theorize that larger sharks with more experience know where to find the best hunting sites, and that size dominance might be a factor. Tracking studies revealed that in about 98 feet of water, great whites swam at a depth of 66 feet and appeared to use their cryptic countershading to enhance predatory opportunities. Another study found that great whites' stomach temperatures were elevated to 77°F in an ambient water temperature of 57°F—a result of their rete mirabile heating systems (see **Chapter 2: Anatomy: Muscles**).

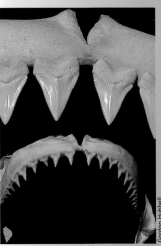

Adult (top) and juvenile great white shark teeth.

Juvenile great whites (less than 6.5 feet) feed on crabs, cephalopods, sharks, rays and bony fish. Adult great whites (at or more than 13 feet) feed on other sharks, rays, bony fish, elephant seals, harbor seals, California sea lions and probably other pinniped species. Great whites have been caught in Hawai'i between December and May—the humpback whale calving season.

NOTES: Danger Rating: High. Although rare in Hawai'i, this shark is always dangerous. In False Bay, South Africa, great whites have been known to attack boats until they sank, and in one instance, the shark actually lept into a boat. Underwater, however, divers have reported great whites who approached them to within a few feet and then retreated without attacking. Only two shark attacks in Hawai'i have been associated with great whites: In 1926, the remains of a man believed to be William Goins were found in the stomach of a great white caught off Kahuku; and in 1969, teeth imprints in Lucius Lee's surfboard indicated that a great white was responsible for biting his leg at Mākaha.

ORDER/FAMILY: Lamniformes/Lamnidae

REFERENCES: Compagno, 1984; Taylor, 1985; Klimley and Ainley, 1996; Goldman, 1997; Goldman and Anderson, 1999; Winter and Cliff, 1999; Boustany et al, 2002.

Shortfin Mako Shark
Isurus oxyrhinchus

(OTHER NAMES: blue pointer, mackeral shark, taupe blau, marrajo dientuso)

SIZE: Birth size is about 2.3 ft.; maximum length 13 ft.

REPRODUCTION: Live birth, aplacental oophagous: no uterine attachment; embryos use up their initial egg yolk, then receive a large number of additional eggs to feed on. Litter size ranges from 4-25. Gestation is thought to last from 15-18 months. Males mature at about 6.4 ft.; females mature at about 9 ft.

HABITAT: A wide-ranging pelagic shark found in all oceans and the Mediterranean and Red Seas from the surface to at least 918 feet. In Hawai'i, this species is captured at depths of 114 to 918 feet. It prefers a water temperature of 62.5°-71.5°F. Three shortfin mako sharks tracked in the colder waters off southern California swam mostly in the mixed layer of the thermocline at 46 to 66 feet. Tagging programs in the Atlantic Ocean report that shortfin mako sharks have been recaptured up to 2,452 nautical miles from their original tagging site.

DESCRIPTION: Short pectoral fins; a very pointed, conical snout with long, dagger-like teeth. The tail lobes are nearly equal in size, and there is a pronounced keel at the base of the tail.

BIOLOGY: An aggressive, active-feeding shark, the shortfin mako is the fastest swimming of all sharks and is capable of reaching 50-mph during short bursts of speed. The California-tagged sharks mentioned in **Habitat** above cruised at an average speed of 0.82-mph. The Atlantic-tagged sharks averaged 17.7 nautical miles per day, although one shark was estimated to have covered 35.7 nautical miles per day. The shortfin mako feeds primarily on bony fish, sharks, squid, sea turtles, and marine mammals.

NOTES: Danger Rating: Moderate. This shark is typically found offshore, but due to its aggressive nature, it should always be considered dangerous. **Economic Impact:** Along with the big-eye and pelagic thresher, the shortfin mako is sold at Honolulu's fish auction. **Outdated Scientific Names:** *Isuropsis glauca.*

ORDER/FAMILY: Lamniformes/Lamnidae

REFERENCES: Compagno, 1984; Casey and Kohler, 1992; Holts and Bedford, 1993; Crow et al., 1996; Nakano et al., 1997.

Longfin Mako Shark
Isurus paucus

(OTHER NAMES: Petit taupe;
Marrajo carite)

SIZE: Birth size about 4 ft.; maximum length possibly exceeding 13.9 ft.

REPRODUCTION: Live birth, aplacental oophagous: no uterine attachment; embryos use up their initial egg yolk, then receive a large number of additional eggs to feed on. Length of gestation is unknown. Litter size ranges from 1-8 pups. Males mature at about 8 ft., females mature at about 9.3 ft.

HABITAT: A wide-ranging pelagic shark found in all oceans from near the surface to at least 328 feet (caught off Brazil to 4,260 feet). No detailed records are available for Hawai'i as this species is not separated from the shortfin mako in fisheries records.

DESCRIPTION: A dark brownish-gray shark with long conical snout, blade-like teeth and a well-developed keel. Large specimens have darker areas on the underside of the body and lower jaw.

BIOLOGY: Frequently caught by commercial longline fishermen

although very little is known about this species. Presumably feeds on squid and bony fish.

NOTES: Danger Rating: Moderate. This shark is found offshore but should be considered dangerous due to its large size. **Economic Impact:** Both longfin and shortfin makos are sold at Honolulu's fish auction.

ORDER/FAMILY: Lamniformes/Lamnidae

REFERENCES: Gilmore, 1983; Compagno, 1984; Casey, 1986; Amorin et al., 1998.

Spongehead Cat Shark
Apristurus spongiceps
(OTHER NAMES: Holbiche tete molle, Pejagato esponjoso)

Sandra Raredon, Smithsonian Institution, NMNH (preserved)

Sandra Raredon, Smithsonian Institution, NMNH (preserved)

Sandra Raredon, Smithsonian Institution, NMNH (preserved)

SIZE: Birth size unknown; female adult from Hawai'i 1.6 ft. Only two spongehead cat sharks have ever been found.

REPRODUCTION: Hawai'i's only egg-laying species: oviparous.

HABITAT: A deep-water, bottom-dwelling shark found only in the Pacific Ocean. Depth range is uncertain but estimated at 1,900 to 4,800 feet. The Hawaiian specimen, on deposit in the U.S. Museum of Natural History, Smithsonian Institution, was caught in 1904 off Bird Island near Laysan Atoll in the Northwestern Hawaiian Islands and was the first of this species to be discovered. The second was captured in 1913 off southern Sulawesi, Indonesia, in the Banda Sea.

DESCRIPTION: Color: dark brown. A thick-bodied shark with a wide head and pleats and grooves around its gill slits.

BIOLOGY: Unknown.

NOTES: Danger Rating: None, due to size and deep-water habitat. **Outdated Scientific Names:** *Catulus spongiceps*

ORDER/FAMILY: Carcharhiniformes/Scyliorhinidae

REFERENCES: Gilbert, 1905; Compagno, 1984.

False Cat Shark
Pseudotriakis microdon
(OTHER NAMES: Requin a longue dorsale,
Musolon de aleta larga)

SIZE: Birth size about 4 ft.; maximum length 10 ft. Males mature at 6.5 ft., females mature at about 7 ft.

REPRODUCTION: Live birth, aplacental oophagous: no uterine attachment; embryo feeds on its own egg yolk, then receives extra eggs during development. Normal litter size: 2, one embryo per uterus.

HABITAT: A pelagic shark found in all oceans, from 650-5,000 feet deep. Hawaiian records of longline sets off the southern and western coasts of O'ahu indicate the false cat shark is found at 1,200 feet. Submersible sightings off southern O'ahu put this shark as deep as 1,600 feet.

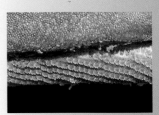

*False cat shark teeth
(preserved, BPBM)*

DESCRIPTION: Color: dark brownish-gray. A large, bulky, soft-bodied shark with catlike eyes and large spiracles. The long first dorsal fin extends virtually all the way from the pectoral to the pelvic fin region.

BIOLOGY: A varied diet includes shrimp, octopus, sharks and bony fish.

(preserved, BPBM)

NOTES: Danger Rating: Minimal, due to its deep-water habitat.

ORDER/FAMILY:
Carcharhiniformes/Pseudotriakidae

REFERENCES: Compagno, 1984; Crow et al., 1996; Yano, 1992.

Bignose Shark
Carcharhinus altimus

(OTHER NAMES: Requin babosse, mendhan miyaru, Tiburon baboso)

John Naughton

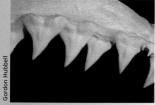

Gordon Hubbell

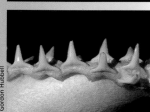

Gordon Hubbell

Upper and lower teeth.

SIZE: Birth size 2-2.5 ft.; maximum length 9.5 ft.

REPRODUCTION: Live birth, placental: embryos develop in the uterus and attach to the uterine lining. Litter size ranges from 3-15 pups. Males mature at just over 6 ft., females mature at just over 6.5 ft.

HABITAT: A pelagic shark found in all oceans and the Mediterranean Sea and Red Sea. This species is probably often misidentified, resulting in reported distribution errors. Worldwide, it has been seen at depths of 82-1,600 feet. Hawaiian records indicate it is caught at anywhere from 88 to 1,200 feet. This wide range of capture depths has led to speculation that the bignose is a vertical migrator.

DESCRIPTION: Color: gray. A large shark with prominent nasal flaps and a high interdorsal ridge.

BIOLOGY: Diet includes crustaceans, squid, sharks, rays and bony fish.

NOTES: Danger Rating: Minimal, due to offshore and deep-water habitat.

ORDER/FAMILY: Carcharhiniformes/Carcharhinidae

REFERENCES: Compagno, 1984; Anderson and Stevens, 1996; Crow et al. 1996.

Top view.
(preserved, BPBM)

Galapagos Shark
Carcharhinus galapagensis
(OTHER NAMES: Requin des Galapagos, Tiburon de Galapagos)

Jack Randall

SIZE: Birth size 2.6 ft.; maximum reported length in Hawai'i 9.8 ft; elsewhere 11.5 ft.

REPRODUCTION: Live birth, placental: embryos develop in the uterus and form an attachment to the uterine lining. Gestation takes 11-12 months. In Hawai'i, litter size ranges from 4-16. Males mature at 6.7-7.8 ft., females mature at 7-8 ft. Both mature at 6-9 years (estimated).

HABITAT: A coastal shark inhabiting all oceans but with a limited distribution—most common around islands from the surface to 600 feet. In Hawai'i, these sharks are most often found in the Northwestern Hawaiian Islands, preferring areas of converging currents and offshore water flow. Juveniles will readily approach fishing and dive boats at Midway Atoll, possibly out of curiosity, and both juveniles and adults have been known to act aggressively towards divers at times. In the main Hawaiian Islands, there is evidence that juveniles, adult females and adult males are segregated by depth (148 feet, 111 feet, and 197 feet, respectively).

DESCRIPTION: Color: brownish-gray on dorsal surface, white underside; the trailing edge of the tail is dusky colored but not black.

BIOLOGY: In Hawai'i, stomach contents have included primarily bony fish, squid, octopus, crustaceans and—as size increases— more rays and smaller sharks.

NOTES: Danger Rating: Moderate. Because of its large size and aggressive/curious nature, the Galapagos shark should be considered potentially dangerous.

ORDER/FAMILY: Carcharhiniformes/Carcharhinidae

REFERENCES: Wass, 1971; Compagno, 1984; DeCrosta et al., 1984; Wetherbee et al., 1996.

Gray Reef Shark
Carcharhinus amblyrhynchos
(OTHER NAMES: grey reef shark, Requin dagsit, Tiburon de arrecifes)

Jack Randall

SIZE: Birth size 20-24 in.; maximum length 6.2 ft. In Hawai'i, researchers estimated that a 5.5 ft. adult was 12-13 years old.

REPRODUCTION: Live birth, placental: embryos develop in the uterus and form an attachment to the uterine lining. Gestation period is 11-12 months. In Hawai'i, litter size ranges from 3-6 pups; years to reproductive maturity: 6-8; males mature at 3.9-4.5 ft; females mature at about 4.1 ft., although the smallest pregnant female was recorded at 4.7 ft.

HABITAT: Primarily a coastal shark found in the Indian and Pacific Oceans, the gray reef shark is reported to circle and dive with submarines. Hawaiian records show it is caught from the surface to 900 feet, although it is most abundant from the surface to 320 feet. In Hawai'i, this shark is more common in the Northwestern Hawaiian Islands than elsewhere and tends to prefer reef areas with rugged terrain and strong currents on the leeward sides of islands. It is a curious shark and can be aggressive at times, especially when alone rather than in a group. It will often assume a warning posture (pectoral fins pointing down, back arched) but rarely attack people. When in an aggressive mode, gray reef sharks have chased experienced divers out of the ocean by biting their dive fins.

DESCRIPTION: Color: gray, with a slight white streak on the back edge of the dorsal fin and a conspicuous black margin on the trailing edge of the tail. No interdorsal ridge.

BIOLOGY: Life span: at least 12 years. Stomach contents studied in Hawai'i consisted of bony fish (85%), octopus and squid (29.5%) and crustaceans (4.9%).

NOTES: Danger Rating: Moderate. Generally not aggressive, but at certain locations and times can be very aggressive.
Outdated Scientific Names: *Carcharias nesiotes*

ORDER/FAMILY: Carcharhiniformes/Carcharhinidae

REFERENCES: Wass, 1971; Compagno, 1984; Radtke and Cailliet, 1984; Wetherbee et al., 1997.

97

Silky Shark
Carcharhinus falciformis
(OTHER NAMES: Requin soyeux, Tiburon jaqueton)

SIZE: Birth size 2.3 to 2.6 ft.; maximum length 10.8 ft. Researchers estimated that a 9.6 ft. female was 22 years old.

REPRODUCTION: Live birth, placental: embryos develop in the uterus and form an attachment to the uterine lining. Gestation lasts 11-12 months; mating and pupping occur throughout the year; normal litter size: 2-15. Years to reproductive maturity: 10-12; males and females mature at about 7.2 ft. Pupping areas in the central Pacific range from the equator (0°) to 15° north latitude.

HABITAT: A pelagic and coastal shark found in all oceans and the Red Sea from the surface to 1,600 ft. Around the Hawaiian Islands, the silky is usually pelagic, rarely appearing in coastal areas.

DESCRIPTION: Color: brownish-gray. A large shark with a small, rounded dorsal fin, an interdorsal ridge and no distinctive markings.

BIOLOGY: The silky feeds on crustaceans, octopus, squid and bony fish. It is commonly caught by commercial longline boats fishing south of the Hawaiian Islands and seems to be associated with schools of tuna.

NOTES: Danger Rating: Minimal, due to its offshore habitat around Hawai'i.

ORDER/FAMILY: Carcharhiniformes/Carcharhinidae

REFERENCES: Compagno, 1984; Last and Stevens, 1994; Bonfil et al., 1993.

Blacktip Shark
Carcharhinus limbatus

(OTHER NAMES: blacktip whaler, Requin borde, Tiburon macuira)

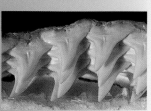

SIZE: Birth size generally 15.7-27.5 in. (In Hawai'i, a recently born speciman with umbilical scar measured 28.5 in.); maximum length 8.4 ft.

REPRODUCTION: Live birth, placental: embryos develop in the uterus and form an attachment to the uterine lining. Gestation period is 11-12 months, and litter size can range from 1-10 pups. In Hawai'i, pupping season is June to July. Worldwide, males mature at 4.5-5.9 ft; females mature at 4.5-6.2 ft. In Hawai'i, males and females mature at about 5.7 ft.

HABITAT: A coastal and pelagic shark found in all oceans and the Mediterranean and Red Seas from the surface to 210 ft. In Hawai'i, it has been caught at depths of 43-210 ft. and pups have been seen in many areas including Kāne'ohe Bay and at Midway Atoll.

DESCRIPTION: Color: gray, with black edges on dorsal and pectoral fins, and a pointed snout.

BIOLOGY: This shark is fairly common around the Hawaiian Islands where its diet consists of octopus, squid and bony fish. Worldwide, examined stomach contents also included crustaceans, sharks, rays and cetaceans (probably scavenged from a dead whale).

NOTES: Danger Rating: Minimal; few reports of aggression.
Outdated Scientific Names: *Carcharias phorcys*

ORDER/FAMILY: Carcharhiniformes/Carcharhinidae

REFERENCES: Compagno, 1984; Crow et al., 1996.

John Naughton

Oceanic Whitetip Shark
Carcharhinus longimanus
(OTHER NAMES: Requin oceanique, Tiburon oceanico)

Tom Fenske

SIZE: Birth size 1.8-2.5 ft.; maximum length 11.5 ft. Researchers estimated that a 6.2 ft. adult was 11 years old.

REPRODUCTION: Live birth, placental; embryos develop in the uterus and form an attachment to the uterine lining. Females probably reproduce every other year, although mating and pupping occur throughout the year, rather than in any particular season. Gestation is estimated at 11-12 months. Normal litter size: 1-15. Years to reproductive maturity: 5-6; males and females mature at about 5.7 ft. Specific pupping areas in the central North Pacific range from the equator to 15° north latitude.

HABITAT: A wide-ranging pelagic shark found in all oceans and the Red Sea. Usually caught from the surface to 500 ft. In Hawai'i, the oceanic whitetip hangs out mostly around the Big Island.

DESCRIPTION: Color: gray, with long, white-tipped pectoral fins and a large white-tipped dorsal fin.

BIOLOGY: The oceanic whitetip is an aggressive and curious shark that will approach and bump divers to assuage its curiosity. It feeds on a wide variety of foods including crustaceans, squid, pelagic stingrays, bony fish, birds, sea turtles, and marine mammals.

Upper-jaw teeth.

NOTES: Danger Rating: Moderate. Can be aggressive if encountered in offshore waters. **Outdated Scientific Names:** *Carcharias insularum*

ORDER/FAMILY: Carcharhiniformes/Carcharhinidae

REFERENCES: Compagno, 1984; Seki et al., 1998.

Blacktip Reef Shark
Carcharhinus melanopterus

(OTHER NAMES: Requin pointes noires, Tiburon de puntas negras; **Hawaiian:** manō pā'ele)

Jack Randall

SIZE: Birth size 19.5 in.; maximum length 4.8 ft. (measured in Hawai'i).

REPRODUCTION: Live birth, placental: embryos develop in the uterus and form an attachment to the uterine lining. Mating to pupping may take 14 months (gestation period has been reported as 8-9 months or up to 14 months). A delay period may occur either after mating and before ovulation (see **Chapter 5: Sex Lives**), or after the fertilized eggs are in the uterus (embryonic diapause). In Hawai'i, pupping season is July to September. Normal litter size: 2-4. Years to reproductive maturity for females: 9. Males mature at about 3 ft; females mature at about 3.2 ft.

HABITAT: A coastal shark found in the Indian and Pacific Oceans and the Mediterranean and Red Seas. In Hawai'i, this species can be seen very close to the coastline and coral reef edge, and because of this, is very susceptible to reef gill netting. No blacktip reef sharks were caught during shark-control programs, which typically fished outside the reef. This shark is found from the surface to 100 ft.

DESCRIPTION: Color: light-brown with large black marks on the first dorsal fin and lower tail tips; no interdorsal ridge.

BIOLOGY: Diet consists of crustaceans, squid, octopus and bony fish. Blacktip reef sharks are often kept in aquariums and can have a drastically different growth rate depending on how much they are fed.

NOTES: Danger Rating: Minimal in Hawai'i. There have been a number of attacks in the vicinity of other Pacific islands where these sharks appear to be more aggressive. To avoid getting bitten by this shark, Pacific islanders have learned to swim rather than walk their canoes over near-surface reefs between atolls (feet and legs look smaller and less intimidating to the shark—therefore easier to bite—than an immersed body). **Outdated Scientific Names:** *Carcharias melanopterus*

ORDER/FAMILY: Carcharhiniformes/Carcharhinidae

REFERENCES: Compagno, 1984; Taylor and Wisner 1989; Last and Stevens, 1994; Sea World of California, personal communication.

Sandbar Shark
Carcharhinus plumbeus
(OTHER NAMES: Requin gris, Tiburon trozo)

Jack Randall

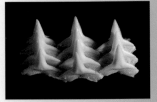

SIZE: In Hawai'i, birth size averages 25 in.; maximum length 6.4 ft.; worldwide maximum length 7.9 ft.

REPRODUCTION: Live birth, placental: embryos develop in the uterus and form an attachment to the uterine lining. Gestation lasts 11-12 months, and females reproduce every other year. In Hawai'i, pupping season is July to September, and litter size ranges from 1-8 pups. Worldwide, litters can be as large as 14 pups. Males mature at 5 ft., females mature at 5.2 ft.

HABITAT: A coastal shark found in all oceans and the Mediterranean and Red Seas from intertidal areas down to 918 ft. Common in Hawai'i, where it is found from 29-912 ft. Depths for male and juvenile sandbar sharks average 367 ft, while females cruise in shallower areas at an average of 223 ft.

DESCRIPTION: Color: gray or light tan. This shark has a high first dorsal fin, strong interdorsal ridge and no distinct markings.

BIOLOGY: Examined stomach contents of Hawai'i's sandbar sharks consisted of bony fish (70%), octopus and squid (27%), crustaceans (18%), and sharks and rays (3%). This species might live up to 30 years.

NOTES: Danger Rating: Minimal. **Outdated Scientific Names:** *Carcharhinus milberti*

ORDER/FAMILY:
Carcharhiniformes/Carcharhinidae

REFERENCES: Wass, 1971; Wass, 1973; Compagno, 1984; Last and Stevens, 1994.

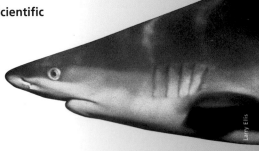

Larry Ellis

Tiger Shark
Galeocerdo cuvier

(OTHER NAMES: Requin tigre commun, Tintorera;
Hawaiian: niuhi)

Jack Randall

Susan H. Rickards

A tiger shark lunges for a black-footed Laysan albatross.

SIZE: Birth size 30-36 in.; maximum length 19.6 ft.; rare over 15 ft.

REPRODUCTION: Live birth, aplacental with one egg. Embryos develop in compartmentalized uteri where they are nourished by their attached yolk sacs and presumably receive nutritive fluids through the uterine lining (see **Chapter 5: Sex Lives: A Good Egg**).
10-82 pups per litter. Females store sperm in the oviducal gland until eggs develop. Ovulation to birth takes 15-16 months. Tiger sharks are thought to reproduce once every three years. In Hawai'i mating occurs in January, ovulation from May-July, and pups are born in Sept.-Oct. of the following year. Years to reproductive maturity: around Hawai'i, 10-12; in other oceans, 7-9. In general, males mature at 9.5-10.6 ft, females mature at 9.3-10 ft.

HABITAT: A wide-ranging species occuring in all tropical and temperate oceans and the Red Sea. Hawaiian fishing records show that tiger sharks have been caught from the surface to 1,200 ft. They can be found along coastlines and up to 365 nautical miles from shore. Tracking studies in the Hawaiian Islands indicate a highly nomadic species with a large home range and the ability to swim 30 miles in 24 hours. While in coastal waters, tracked tiger sharks often swim close to reef drop-offs at depths of 195 to 260 ft., a depth usually above the thermocline.

DESCRIPTION: Broadly rounded snout with distinctive curved, serrated teeth. Strong spotting pattern in young sharks, fading to stripes and then to almost solid light gray in adults.

BIOLOGY: Tiger sharks have been called the garbage can of the sea due to their highly varied diet. Stomach contents have included sacks of coal, a bag of potatoes, raincoats, a driver's license, and a feather-coated chicken coop. The Hawaiian tiger shark's nutritive diet consists of squid, octopus, crustaceans,

Newborn tiger shark pup

sharks, rays, bony fish, green sea turtles, birds and dolphins, although anything washed into the sea is fair game. The stomach of a 10-foot female found in Kāne'ohe Bay contained parts of a sandbar shark, turtle shell, rat, trumpetfish, and isopods (type of crustacean). Inspections of other tiger shark stomachs revealed parts of horses, cows, goats, sheep, dogs, cats, mongooses, rats and human remains. (For the specifics of a tiger shark's diet, see **Chapter 4: Feeding Habits**.) A tiger shark's average
swimming speed is 2.4 mph.

NOTES: Danger Rating: High. Hawai'i, where tiger sharks are common, averages 1-2 attacks per year—a relatively low number for this dangerous shark. **Outdated Scientific Names:** *Galeocerdo tigrinus*

ORDER/FAMILY: Carcharhiniformes/Carcharhinidae

REFERENCES: Compagno, 1984; DeCosta et al., 1984; Polovina and Lau, 1994; Crow, 1995; Lowe et al., 1996; Holland et al., 1999.

Blue Shark
Prionace glauca
(OTHER NAMES: Tiburon azul, Peau bleue, Blue whaler)

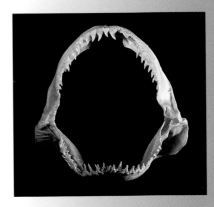

SIZE: Birth size 14-20 in.; maximum length 12.5 ft.

REPRODUCTION: Live birth, placental: embryos develop in the uterus and form an attachment to the uterine lining. Litters range from 4-135 pups, but the average is 40-80. Gestation is 9-12 months, and mating takes place during the summer in the vicinity of 20°-30° north latitude in the North Pacific; pregnant females, who are thought to mate and pup every two years, travel north, and pups are born in May and June at 35°-45° north latitude, moving south to adult feeding areas as they mature (for details on blue shark movements, see **Chapter 5: Sex Lives**). Both sexes reach reproductive maturity at 5-6 years. Males mature between 6-9 ft., females mature between 7-10.6 ft.

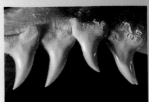

John Naughton

HABITAT: In the Atlantic and Pacific Oceans, this pelagic shark vertically migrates between the surface and 1,800 feet during the day, and between the surface and 600 feet at night. Near islands, the blue shark remains offshore during summer months, but appears to move closer to shore at twilight in the spring to search for food, returning to the open ocean before sunrise. The blue shark is a long-distance traveler, often migrating from the east coast of the U.S. to the edge of Europe in the Atlantic, throughout the Pacific, and occasionally to regions below the equator. Less abundant near the equator, this shark is most populous in northern or southern regions.

DESCRIPTION: Color: bluish gray. A large, slender shark with pointed snout, long pectoral fins, and anterior dorsal fin behind the pectoral fins.

BIOLOGY: Diet consists of bony fish, sea birds, marine mammals and squid, which appears to be a major source of food and one reason for this shark's daily vertical migrations. Average swimming speed is about one mph.

NOTES: Danger Rating: Minimal, due to its offshore habitat. **Economic Impact:** In Hawai'i, blue shark fins accounted for a sizable chunk of the profitable finning trade.

ORDER/FAMILY: Carcharhiniformes/Carcharhinidae

REFERENCES: Sciarrotta and Nelson, 1977; Tricas, 1979; Pratt, 1979; Compagno, 1984; Carey and Scharold, 1990; Nakano and Seki, 2001.

Whitetip Reef Shark
Triaenodon obesus

(OTHER NAMES: whitetip shark, Requin corail,
Tiburon coralero nato; **Hawaiian:** manō lālākea)

Jack Randall

SIZE: Birth size 1.7-1.9 ft. Maximum length 5.6 ft.

REPRODUCTION: Live birth, placental; embryos
develop in the uterus and form an attachment to the
uterine lining. Gestation lasts a little more than a year,
and females reproduce every 2 or 3 years. Mating
has been observed in June, and pups are born the
following June-July. Years to reproductive maturity:
7-9; males and females mature at about 3.4 ft.
Normal litter size: 1-5.

HABITAT: A coastal shark found in the Indian and Pacific
Oceans and the Red Sea, particularly in the vicinity
of coral reefs, at depths of 26-131 ft. (although it has been
recorded as deep as 1,000 ft.). This shark can be observed
throughout the Hawaiian Islands resting in caves, and it may
take up residence in the same cave for extended periods.

DESCRIPTION: Color: gray. Slightly flat-headed with small
white tips on the tops of the first and second dorsal and tail fins.

BIOLOGY: The whitetip reef is a very active nocturnal predator
that will swim into crevices in rocks and coral heads to search
for food. It's also alert during the day in the vicinity of divers
who are spear-fishing and will frequently steal speared fish.
Diet includes octopus, crustaceans and bony fish.

NOTES: Danger Rating: Minimal under
normal and non-threatening conditions.

ORDER/FAMILY: Carcharhiniformes/Carcharhinidae

REFERENCES: Compagno, 1984; Uchida et al., 1990;
Kajiura, personal communication.

Jack Randall

Scalloped Hammerhead Shark

Sphyrna lewini
(OTHER NAMES: Requin-marteau halicorne, Cornuda comun; **Hawaiian:** manō kihikihi)

John Naughton

SIZE: Birth size 16-20 in.; maximum length 12 ft.

REPRODUCTION: Live birth, placental: embryos develop in the uterus and form an attachment to the uterine lining. Gestation period is 11-12 months, and litter size ranges from 15-31 pups. In Kāne'ohe Bay, pupping takes place from May to July. Males mature at just under 5 ft., females mature at about 6.5 ft. Age at maturity has been calculated at 4 years in Taiwan, but is 10-15 years in the Gulf of Mexico and Hawai'i where the growth rate is slower.

HABITAT: A coastal and pelagic shark found in all oceans and the Mediterranean and Red Seas. In Hawai'i, the scalloped hammerhead has been recorded in shallow areas just offshore and as deep as 900 feet (caught in a gill net)—the depth world record for this shark species.

DESCRIPTION: Color: gray. This shark has a flattened hammer-like head with a central indentation.

BIOLOGY: Adults live offshore and come into the shallower waters of Hilo Bay, Kāne'ohe Bay, Waimea Bay and other areas around the Hawaiian Islands to pup. Juveniles tracked in Kāne'ohe Bay stay near the bottom in deeper parts of the bay and at night disperse to other areas, presumably to feed. Juveniles feed primarily in bottom areas, choosing a diet of shrimp and bony fish. Adults eat bony fish, squid, sharks and rays.

NOTES: Danger Rating: Moderate; reported to attack people in offshore waters.

ORDER/FAMILY: Carcharhiniformes/Sphyrnidae

REFERENCES: Clarke, 1971; Compagno, 1984; Branstetter, 1987; Chen et al., 1990; Holland et al., 1993; Last and Stevens, 1994; Crow et al., 1996; Bush, 1998.

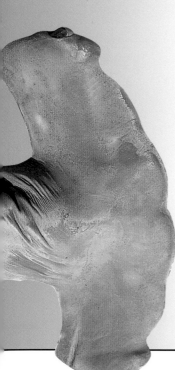

Left: Head scallops are evident on this juvenile shark (preserved, BPBM).

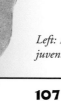

Smooth Hammerhead Shark

Sphyrna zygaena

(OTHER NAMES: common hammerhead, Requin-marteau commun, cornuda cruz; **Hawaiian:** manō kihikihi)

SIZE: Birth size 19.5-24 in.; maximum length 11.5 ft.

REPRODUCTION: Live birth, placental: embryos develop in the uterus and form an attachment to the uterine lining. Gestation period is 11-12 months, and litter size ranges from 20-50 pups. Males mature at about 7.5 ft., females mature at about 8.5 ft.

The catch includes a smooth hammerhead, second shark from front.

HABITAT: A coastal and pelagic shark found in all oceans and the Mediterranean Sea from the surface to 223 ft. In Hawai'i, juvenile smooth hammerheads ranging in size from 5.3-7 ft. have been caught at depths of 108-223 ft.

DESCRIPTION: Color: gray. This shark has a flattened hammer-like head without a median indentation.

BIOLOGY: Diet in Hawai'i consists of crustaceans, squid and bony fish. Worldwide, it is reported to also eat sharks and rays.

NOTES: Danger Rating: Probably minimal, but could be potentially dangerous offshore. This species' presence in Hawai'i has yet to be verified.

ORDER/FAMILY: Carcharhiniformes/Sphyrnidae

REFERENCES: Compagno, 1984; Last and Stevens, 1994; Crow et al. 1996.

Wayward Wanderer: Basking Shark

Occasionally, a shark that's not a resident of Hawai'i will arrive in the Islands by accident. Such was the case on Monday, June 20, 1983 when a 27-foot-8-inch-long basking shark *(Cetorhinus maximus)* washed up on the rocky beach at Pilale Bay, Maui. John Naughton of the National Marine Fisheries Service, and Fred Ball, a State of Hawai'i biologist for the island of Maui, examined the unusual shark on June 21. Its dorsal fin alone was 4 feet 2 inches high, and each clasper measured 5 feet 4 inches in length.

Beached basking sharks have been called sea serpents because of their strange appearance: long body, pointed nose and large, frilled gills—especially noticeable as the carcass deteriorates on the beach.

This wayward wanderer remains the only one of its species to be reported in Hawai'i.

Basking shark teeth.

A Case of Mistaken Identity: Tope Shark

Blame the shark census takers: Sometimes a shark is identified as a Hawai'i resident when it is not. A researcher named Steindachner reported seeing a tope shark (*Galeorhinus galeus,* previously known as *Galeus japonicus*) at Laysan Atoll in 1901. However this was most likely an inaccurate identification. We don't know what shark he saw, but the tope shark is an abundant, coastal-pelagic species whose habitat ranges from the surface to more than 1,500 feet, and if it occurred in Hawai'i, other tope sharks would surely have been seen since 1901.

RAYS
OF HAWAI'I

Torpedo Ray
Torpedo sp.

(OTHER NAMES: electric ray) (At present, this species has not been formally identified, therefore all information in this description pertains to Hawaiian specimens)

Courtesy of HURL

Embryo (preserved, BPBM).

SIZE: Birth size unknown. Seven specimens have either been observed from submersibles or collected in trawls. Those from trawls measured 8.3-17 in. in total length (from the tip of the head to the end of the tail).

REPRODUCTION: Live birth, presumably aplacental with the embryo receiving nourishment from uterine milk. No other details are available.

HABITAT: Observed from a Hawai'i Undersea Research Laboratory (HURL) submersible, this ray has been sighted swimming near the Big Island close to the sea floor at a depth of 1,089 feet, and has been caught in trawls at depths of 300 to 1,562 feet off Maui, O'ahu (Barbers Point), and in the Kalohi Channel between Moloka'i and Lana'i.

DESCRIPTION: Color: brown, with a broad oval disc body that houses two electric organs, small eyes, two dorsal fins and a short tail with no spine.

BIOLOGY: Stuns its prey with electric shock. No information on diet is available.

NOTES: Danger Rating: Minimal, due to its deep-water habitat.

ORDER/FAMILY: Torpediniformes/Torpedinidae

REFERENCES: Struhsaker, 1973; Chave and Mundy, 1994; Arnold Suzumoto, personal conversation; Bishop Museum records.

Giant Stingaree

Plesiobatis daviesi

(OTHER NAMES: deep-water stingray)

Courtesy of HURL

SIZE: Birth size is unknown; maximum disc width 5 ft.

REPRODUCTION: No recorded information. Presumed to be live bearing with offspring receiving nourishment from a yolk sac. It is not known if this species provides uterine milk. Number of pups observed in Hawai'i: 4.

*Tail spine
(preserved, BPBM)*

HABITAT: Found over sandy sea floors 2,230 feet deep in the Indian and Pacific Oceans. In Hawai'i, this ray has been captured in trawls, gill nets, and on bottom-fishing lines at depths of 600 to 1,300 feet.

DESCRIPTION: **Color:** gray-black on top; white ventral surface with dark edges. This ray has a moderately elongated snout and thick tail, which becomes laterally flattened in the region beyond the tail spine and ends at a pointed tip.

BIOLOGY: Eats octopus, shrimp, crab and lizardfish. Observers in Hawai'i Undersea Research Laboratory (HURL) submersibles have seen this species creating billowing plumes of sand while feeding on the sea floor, leaving behind cylindrical depressions in the sandy bottom.

NOTES: **Danger Rating:** None, due to its deep-water habitat. **Outdated Scientific Names:** *Urotrygon daviesi*

ORDER/FAMILY: Myliobatiformes/Plesiobatidae

REFERENCES: Clarke, 1972; Struhsaker, 1973; Last and Stevens, 1994; Chave and Malahoff, 1998.

*Left: Dorsal surface
(preserved, BPBM);
right: Ventral surface
(preserved, BPBM)*

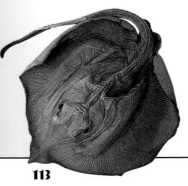

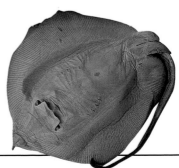

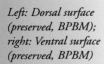

113

Sixgill Stingray
Hexatrygon bickelli

(Five species of Hexatrygon have been described in the research literature, but only one is recognized worldwide. Because identification descriptions are in question, all material presented here relates to the Hawaiian species)

SIZE: Birth size: one fetus was measured at 10.2" disc width. One captured post-birth specimen was measured at 12.6 in. disc width.

REPRODUCTION: Little is known except litter size: 4 pups; and one female was mature at 33 in. disc width.

HABITAT: Found over sandy sea floors and smooth, hard-rock sediments. Observers in Hawai'i Undersea Research Laboratory submersibles have seen this species down to a depth of 3,280 feet.

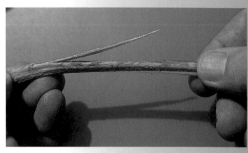

Tail spine (preserved, BPBM).

DESCRIPTION: Color: Brown-black on top, a paler snout, and a white ventral surface with blackish margins (edges). This ray has a long, pointed snout; a short, spined tail; and soft muscle.

BIOLOGY: The sixgill stingray rests on the sea floor and is capable of swimming for prolonged periods.

NOTES: Danger Rating: None, due to its deep-water habitat.
Outdated Scientific Names: *Hexatrygon longirostris*

ORDER/FAMILY: Myliobatiformes/Hexatrygonidae

REFERENCES: Struhsaker, 1973; Last and Stevens, 1994; Stehmann and Shcherbachev, 1995; Chave and Malahoff, 1998; Heemstra, personal communication; Compagno, personal communication.

Below—left: Dorsal surface (preserved, BPBM); right: Ventral surface (preserved, BPBM)

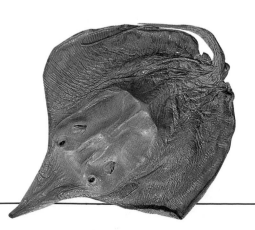
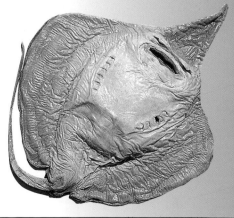

Diamond Stingray
Dasyatis dipterura
(OTHER NAMES: Hawaiian stingray;
Hawaiian: lupe, hīhīmanu)

Arrow points to dorsal fold behind tail spine (preserved).

SIZE: Birth size 7.4 in. disc width.
Maximum size at least 3.2 ft. disc width.

REPRODUCTION: Live birth, aplacental with uterine milk: embryos receive nourishment from one egg yolk and uterine milk. Females mature at 2.2 ft. disc width and give birth during summer after 9 months of embryonic diapause (during which eggs lay idle in the uterus after fertilization) and 3 months of embryo development.

HABITAT: A coastal, bottom-dwelling ray found off Hawai'i, California, and Mexico to Peru at depths to 55 ft.

DESCRIPTION: Color: brownish-black dorsal surface and pale ventral surface. This ray has both a dorsal and ventral fold on its tail.

BIOLOGY: Diet probably consists of crabs, shrimps and bony fish.

NOTES: Danger Rating: Minimal, as this ray is seldom encountered, but it does have a venomous tail spine.
Outdated Scientific Names: *Dasyatis brevis, Dasyatis hawaiensis*

ORDER/FAMILY: Myliobatiformes/Dasyatidae

REFERENCES: Jordan and Evermann, 1905; Nishida and Nakaya, 1990; Mariano-Melenlez and Villavicencio-Garayzor, 1995; Eschmeyer, 1998.

Dorsal surface (preserved).

Sandra Raredon, Smithsonian Institution, NMNH

Brown Stingray
Dasyatis lata
(OTHER NAMES: Hawaiian stingray;
Hawaiian: lupe, hīhīmanu)

SIZE: Birth size is unknown; may reach 5 ft. disc width.

REPRODUCTION: Live birth, aplacental with uterine milk:
Each embryo receives yolk from an individual egg and
uterine milk from mother. Litter size ranges from 3 to 4
young and pups are born in summer. Males mature at 3 ft.
disc width, females mature around 3.7 ft. disc width.

*An aquarist feeds a brown
stingray at Sea Life Park.*

HABITAT: Known only from Taiwan and Hawai'i in the
Pacific Ocean, this ray prefers a sandy sea-floor habitat and
is abundant in Kāne'ohe Bay, O'ahu. In Hawai'i it has been
caught from 1 to 700 feet.

DESCRIPTION: Color: brownish-black. The disc is slightly
wider than long, and this ray has a pronounced snout at
its front end and a tail covered with tubercules.

BIOLOGY: A bottom feeder, the brown stingray eats crab,
shrimp and bony fish.

Jaw and flattened teeth.

NOTES: Danger Rating: Minimal. Beachgoers in shallow
water are in some danger of being stung by this ray's venomous spine if they step on young rays buried in the sand.
Outdated Scientific Names: *Dasyatis sciera, Dasyatis latus*

ORDER/FAMILY: Myliobatiformes/Dasyatidae

REFERENCES: Struhsaker, 1973; Nishida and Nakaya, 1990.

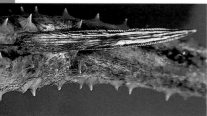

*Above: Brown stingray
tail spine.*

*Right: Snorkeler and
friend in the stingray
lagoon at Sea Life Park.*

Teeth.

Pelagic Stingray
Pteroplatytrygon violacea
(OTHER NAMES: Violet stingray, Guilers stingray)

SIZE: Birth size 7.4 in. disc width. Reported to reach 2.6 ft. disc width.

REPRODUCTION: Live birth, aplacental with uterine milk: Each embryo receives yolk from an individual egg and uterine milk from mother. Males are mature at 1.1 ft. disc width, females are mature at 1.3-1.6 ft. disc width, with males remaining much smaller than females. Litter size might range from 4-7 pups.

HABITAT: This open-ocean ray is found in very deep water, far above the sea floor. In Hawai'i, it is frequently caught by long-line tuna fishermen, and the only confirmed depth catch record is 328 ft.

DESCRIPTION: Color: blackish-brown dorsal and brownish-black ventral surfaces. This is the only ray with dark underside.

BIOLOGY: Reported diet consists of squid, crustaceans, bony fish and possibly jellyfish.

NOTES: Danger Rating: Minimal, due to offshore, deep-water habitat. However this ray's tail spine is venomous and should be avoided. **Outdated Scientific Names:** *Dasyatis violacea*

ORDER/FAMILY: Myliobatiformes/Dasyatidae

Below—left:
Ventral surface;
right: Dorsal surface.

REFERENCES: Coles, 1916; Boggs, 1992; Last and Stevens, 1994; Yano et al., 1999; Mollet, personal communication.

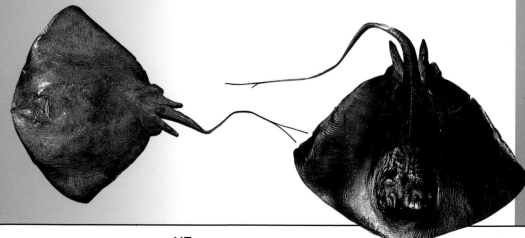

Spotted Eagle Ray
Aetobatus narinari
(OTHER NAMES: bonnet ray, duck-billed ray;
Hawaiian: hīhīmanu, lupe)

SIZE: Birth size: 10-20 in. disc width;
wing span can reach 6 ft.

REPRODUCTION: Live birth, aplacental with uterine milk:
Only the left ovary is functional, and embryos develop only
in the left uterus where they receive milk from one-inch-long
uterine villi. These rays are thought to mature in 4-6 years,
with females maturing at 4.6 ft. disc width. Liter size ranges
from 1-4 young. In Hawai'i, spotted eagle rays are born in
October, November and December in Pearl Harbor and
Kāne'ohe Bay, O'ahu; and on the leeward side of Moloka'i.
Courtship behavior has been observed at Enewetok Atoll in
the Marshall Islands from October through December. During
the birthing process, these rays have been seen leaping from
the water and dropping their young in midair.

Upper jaw tooth plate.

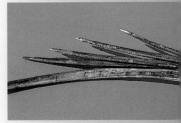

Tail spines.

HABITAT: A coastal ray found in the Atlantic, Indian and Pacific Oceans, this species ranges throughout the Hawaiian Island chain to at least Midway Atoll and prefers shallow water—sometimes only inches deep—and the edge of freshwater runoffs. Eagle rays feed in soft sand sediments, frequently digging visible pits on the sandy sea floor.

DESCRIPTION: A stylishly decorated ray. **Color:** black on top and dotted with white spots; white underneath with a black, geometric maze pattern on the underside of each wing; a flexible, pointed snout.

BIOLOGY: Spotted eagle rays feed primarily on oysters, clams, crabs, shrimp and worms.

NOTES: Danger Rating: Minimal. This ray usually retreats when humans enter its habitat, but its barbed tail spine (some have multiple spines) can pose a danger if touched. **Economic Impact:** There may be some economic impact related to tourism since these rays are on display at Sea Life Park and at the Big Island's Four Seasons Resort at Hualalai. **Outdated Scientific Names:** *Stoasodon narinari*

ORDER/FAMILY: Myliobatiformes/Myliobatidae

REFERENCES: Coles, 1913; Gudger, 1914; Tricas, 1980; Uchida et al., 1990; Last and Stevens, 1994.

Manta Ray
Manta birostris
(OTHER NAMES: manta; **Hawaiian:** hāhālua)

SIZE: Birth size is not known for sure but estimated at 3 ft. wingspan; adult measured to 22 ft. wingspan

REPRODUCTION: Live birth, aplacental with uterine milk. Litter size: 1-2 in the left uterus. Females with an 11 ft. wing span are reported mature. Observers witnessing manta ray courtship off the Ogasawara Islands, Japan, reported two males chasing a female and biting the rear of her left wing. One of the males rotated into a belly-to-belly position, and mating lasted 60 or 90 seconds.

HABITAT: Along the Kona Coast of the Big Island at depths of 10-120 feet. Dive groups and visitors to the seaside terrace of the Mauna Kea Beach Hotel can see manta rays feeding at night. However, not much is known about their movements and habitat.

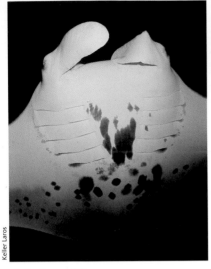

Keller Laros

Michael Connolly

*Lefty shows off her
drooping cephalic horn.*

DESCRIPTION: Color: grayish-blue to greenish-brown on the dorsal surface with pale-silver shoulder patches. The white ventral surface, often marked with black blotches, is edged with a gray margin. Blotches are used to identify individual rays, and based on body size, shape and blotches, dive master Keller Laros has identified 55 manta rays in the vicinity of Kona. One ray, nicknamed Lefty, can be recognized by her bent left cephalic horn. Laros first saw her off the Kona Surf Hotel in 1979, and she has been seen regularly since then.

BIOLOGY: Manta rays are filter feeders and trap food using gill rakers, although they have tiny teeth not used in feeding. Their diet of plankton consists of copepods, mysid shrimp, crab larvae, mollusc larvae and fish eggs.

NOTES: Danger Rating: None; filter-feeding ray; occasionally gets tangled up in fishing or anchor lines (see **Chapter 12: Wild Encounters**). **Economic Impact:** Ecotourism—diving with rays off Kona.

ORDER/FAMILY: Myliobatiformes/Mobulidae

REFERENCES: Coles, 1916; Last and Stevens, 1994; Yano et al., 1999; Eric Beyer, manuscript.

*Star-shaped head scales
(preserved, BPBM).*

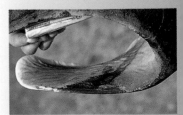

*A cephalic horn (lower part of photo)
(preserved, BPBM) helps funnel
plankton into the manta ray's
mouth. Pencil-point-sized teeth in
the mouth (above fingers) are not
used in feeding.*

Spinetail Devil Ray

Mobula japonica

(OTHER NAMES:
cubanadelorno blanco)

A spinetail devil ray's cephalic horns can be rolled up when not in use for feeding (preserved, BPBM).

SIZE: Birth size about 33 in. disc width; maximum size 10 ft. disc width.

REPRODUCTION: Live birth, aplacental with uterine milk. From observations in the Gulf of California, mating takes place in June and July. A single pup is born from the left uterus. Females are mature at about 6.5 ft. disc width.

HABITAT: Observed near the sea floor in 60-feet of water off Makena, Maui.

DESCRIPTION: Color: bluish-black on the dorsal surface with white crescent patches on the wings; white ventral surface with dark splotches. Although, like the manta ray, the spinetail devil ray is a filter feeder and uses cephalic horns to direct food into its mouth, unlike the manta, its mouth is recessed on the underside of its head, rather than terminal. The first reported specimen was brought to the Honolulu fish market in 1924 and offered for sale. Further verification of this species is in order.

BIOLOGY: Diet consists of euphausid shrimp, copepods and crustacean larvae.

NOTES: Danger Rating: None, due to its offshore habitat and filter-feeding behavior.

ORDER/FAMILY: Myliobatiformes/Mobulidae

REFERENCES: Fowler, 1927; Notarbartolo-DiSciara, 1988; Pauline Fiene-Severns, personal communication.

Recessed mouth (preserved, BPBM).

Tail spine (center of photo) (preserved, BPBM).

Makali'i, the first HURL submersible, prepares to lift off from its platform.

CHAPTER 7

SCIENCE AND SHARKS

Data collection is an important part of scientific research.

Is shark cartilage an effective treatment for cancer? Does shark-liver oil boost the human immune system? Why did 50 people die after eating a bull shark? And how do scientists go about studying sharks to find answers to these and other questions? In this chapter, we'll look at sharks and science—from shark tagging and tracking methods to the shark's impact on medical research. Along the way, don't be surprised if we debunk a few myths and reach some surprising conclusions. First, however, let's take a historical look at scientific efforts to understand the Hawaiian shark's domain.

Stephen M. Kajiura

Measuring a viper dogfish shark.

Weighing a shortfin mako shark.

Early Hawaiians fished with handmade spears.

Discovering a Shark's World

- Exploration of Hawai'i's undersea environment began when early Hawaiians set out with canoes, traps, nets and spears to hunt for food. Understanding life in the sea was essential if fishermen were to be successful and sustain their families and communities.

- In the early 1900s the United States Fish Commission conducted the first large-scale assessment of the Hawaiian Islands' aquatic resources.

- The advent of scuba equipment in the 1940s allowed divers to remain submerged and observe the ocean's ecology to a depth of about 200 feet.

HURL submersible Pisces V is lowered into the water.

- The development of submersibles gave ocean researchers a new tool for scientific exploration. These underwater laboratories began to map Hawai'i's ocean-floor topography around 1965. Then in the 1970s and 80s, the University of Hawai'i's submersible, Makali'i, made routine dives to 1,300 feet. In 1986 the U.H.'s Hawai'i Undersea Research Laboratory refitted the submersible Pisces V for exploration at extended depths of up to 6,500 feet. This seven-foot-diameter submarine has room for a pilot and two observers and can stay submerged for up to 70 hours, although a typical dive lasts six to eight hours. Submersible surveys allow extensive sampling of deep-sea organisms and produce revealing photographs of the deep-sea environment.

A mosaic gulper shark swims past a HURL submersible's collection baskets.

- Another research tool, the rebreather (an oxygen/nitrogen/helium breathing tank with no exhaust bubbles), has allowed free-swimming divers to reach depths of 400 feet and get much closer to sharks and rays than they can with conventional scuba and its noisy bubbles. Richard Pyle, a Bishop Museum biologist who first experimented with the rebreather in shallow waters off Electric Beach near the Leeward Coast's Kahe Point, was surprised to find more than sixteen sandbar sharks milling around just inches from his head, ignoring him as if he were a rock on the sea floor. The sharks disappeared, however, when a group of scuba divers approached. Pyle had come to this spot hundreds of times—always with scuba equipment—without seeing a single shark.

Studying Sharks
Tagging and Technology

Following a series of shark attacks in Hawai'i in the early 1990s, public outcry demanded that the guilty sharks be hunted and killed. The only problem: finding out which sharks were responsible for the attacks. Common wisdom at the time said that a shark patrols a certain territory—a stretch of offshore reef, for example—and can always be found there. As a result, dozens of sharks were killed in an effort to make the offshore areas around Hawai'i safe for swimmers, snorkelers, divers and surfers. Since then, tagging studies have revealed that some of Hawai'i's sharks—tigers in particular—do not stay in one area. Many have far-reaching home ranges that include the span between islands and beyond.

Containing contact information if a shark is re-caught, this red-and-green I.D. tag is attached to the muscle by a v-shaped dart. The cylindrical transmitter—hidden inside a fish and swallowed by the shark, or inserted into the body cavity—allows researchers to track a shark electronically.

To find out how far sharks range, researchers first catch and identify a shark by securing a coded dart tag in the muscle, or a teflon or plastic tag on the dorsal fin. According to studies done with the long-lived tope shark, this tag can stay in place for forty years—more than a lifetime for most sharks. If a tagged shark is

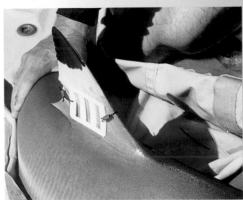

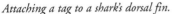

Attaching a tag to a shark's dorsal fin.

A teflon tag on a blacktip reef shark's dorsal fin.

caught, the coded tag asks the fisherman to contact the tagger who then records the size of the animal, the location of capture and the code information. With this data, long-term and migrational movements can be identified and analyzed. The results of such studies show that, although some sharks remain in fairly limited geographical areas, others, such as the tiger, travel between islands. And still others (i.e. blue and mako) might be recaptured several thousand miles from the original tagging site.

Below—top: Ian "Shark" Gordon steadies a juvenile Galapagos shark during author Gerald Crow's Midway Atoll shark-tagging class; bottom: Gordon gets ready to release a tagged shark.

Since the advent of high-tech electronic transmitters and receivers, researchers can examine swimming patterns and behavior by following sharks for several days at a time. Dr. Kim Holland at the University of Hawai'i's Hawai'i Institute of Marine Biology at Coconut Island (O'ahu) who has electronically tracked tiger sharks since 1993—many of them continuously for up to fifty hours—has learned some interesting facts: After being tagged, the sharks typically swam into deeper water offshore at an average rate of 2.4 mph and spent the majority of time at depths of 131 to 328 feet, although some descended to at least 1,110 feet. From these tracks, it's apparent that Hawai'i's tiger sharks are wide-ranging predators with extensive foraging areas.

Other notable studies include the National Marine Fisheries Service's Atlantic Ocean cooperative shark-tagging program, which tagged more than 128,000 sharks between 1962 and 1995. And author Gerald Crow is currently conducting a multi-year tagging project at Midway Atoll in the Northwestern Hawaiian Islands. This study tracks the movement patterns of the atoll's resident Galapagos and gray reef sharks between fishing and diving areas to determine how human activity affects shark behavior.

The latest generation of high-tech tags takes stored information from the transmitter carried by a shark and downloads it to listening stations that activate whenever the tagged shark swims

Betsy Rasmussen

Above: After the hook is removed, this shark will be tagged and its growth rings marked with tetracycline.

nearby. Sharks can also be followed by satellite. Some blue, mako, great white and whale sharks have been fitted with transmitters that download data to a nearby satellite when the antenna breaks the surface of the ocean. Infrared images from satellites can also allow us to predict water-temperature patterns that affect shark distribution.

Tagging sharks can help biologists determine a shark's age in the same way a tree is aged—by counting its growth rings. If a tagged shark is injected with a marker such as tetracycline—which stains growth rings in the shark's backbone—and then recaptured several years later, its age and growth rate can be determined by counting the number of yearly growth rings following the stained ring, and measuring the increase in body size since initial tagging.

Fishery Records

Another source of data proving useful for the scientific study of sharks comes from Hawai'i's commercial longline fishery. Fishery records, maintained by the National Marine Fisheries Service (NMFS) and detailed in logbooks by longline fishermen and NMFS observers on fishing boats, provide valuable information about the number of sharks caught, the type of fishing gear used and the catch location and depth, all of which helps researchers understand the distribution of offshore and wide-ranging shark species. (see **Chapter 10: Fisheries**)

Greg Cailliet, Moss Landing Marine Laboratories

Above: Backbone rings can indicate a shark's age.

Right: Fishing boats like these carry NMFS observers who keep track of the number and types of sharks caught.

Right: Author Gerald Crow measures a 7-foot-5-inch blue shark on a Honolulu Harbor pier.

Museum and Aquarium Collections

Although rarely seen by the viewing public, museum shark and ray collections (preserved in alcohol and stored in glass jars and other containers in a controlled environment) can also be a valuable source of data for scientific study. The Ichthyology Collection at Bishop Museum in Honolulu maintains a detailed reference collection for researchers verifying specimen-identity and geographic-location records.

The Waikīkī Aquarium Shark Gallery provides an opportunity for both scientists and families to learn about sharks and rays.

Aquariums such as the Waikīkī Aquarium also play a vital role in efforts to understand sharks and rays. Researchers often study aquarium animals to learn more about them. Tank displays allow viewers to come face to face with live sharks and rays and observe their behavior in a safe environment. Informational displays-videos, teeth and skeleton samples, sharkskin touch pads, and (in Hawai'i) exhibits that demonstrate how the early Hawaiians used all parts of a shark—demystify sharks and help us appreciate their relationship to us and to the ocean environment. (see **Chapter 8: Sharks and Rays in Aquariums**).

We may be able to benefit from shark research.

Shark Products and Medicine

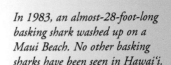

Although still feared, sharks could, in some ways, eventually come to be known as our allies. The possibility that we can benefit from sharks is an assumption rooted in history, as shark products have fallen in and out of favor over the years.

In 1983, an almost-28-foot-long basking shark washed up on a Maui Beach. No other basking sharks have been seen in Hawai'i.

Shark Liver Oil: Vitamin A and Squalene

Two of the first shark products, other than meat, were fins and liver oil. In the 1790s, liver oil from Australia's sand tiger sharks filled household lamps while the fins found ready buyers in Asia. In 1924 a basking-shark fishery began operations in Monterey, California to take advantage of this shark's large liver, which in a 30-foot basking shark might weigh 700 to 2,000 pounds and produce 60 to 70 gallons of oil. The carcass was ground up for livestock feed, dog biscuits, chicken feed and fertilizer. But

Sharks such as this crocodile can adjust the concentrations of their liver oils, which are rich in vitamin A, for more or less buoyancy.

the product most in demand—liver oil—was marketed in the 1920s as "Nature's Own Tonic" because it contained two valuable compounds: squalene and vitamin A.

Before World War II, pharmaceutical companies in America extracted vitamin A from Norway's vast supply of cod-liver oil. But when German troops overran Norway, the supply of this vital commodity was cut off. In San Francisco, an enterprising fish broker, Tano Guaragnella, heard about the need for sources of vitamin A. On a hunch, he took the liver of a spiny dogfish shark (*Squalus acanthias*) to a chemist for analysis and found that it contained ten times the vitamin A content of cod-liver oil. Approaching fishermen on the docks, he offered them $25 per ton of dogfish. They thought he was crazy but supplied him with the shark, which was plentiful in their fishing grounds. One day he noticed that the liver of a soupfin shark (*Galeorhinus galeus*) appeared considerably larger than that of the dogfish, and the subsequent chemist's analysis revealed that it was one hundred times richer in vitamin A than cod-liver oil. Again he approached the fishermen, offering them $40 a ton for soupfin shark. But this time, word leaked out about the enormous profits in "gray gold"—high-priced liver oil from gray sharks—and the new Gold Rush was on. Gray-gold auctions soon sprang up and sparked bidding wars. The price for sharks—a previously worthless catch—went from $40 a ton to $1,500 a ton at the height of the market, when 75% of the vitamin A consumed in the U.S. came from shark-liver oil. This boom in shark-liver vitamin A sales faltered in 1950 when synthetic vitamin A arrived on the market.

Squalene, on the other hand, was peddled as an elixir for rheumatism and burns, an antiseptic for cuts, as cough medication, a laxative, a general tonic and an expensive beauty cream. Recently, updated image marketing for this shark-liver extract has resulted in new health-aid buzz phrases claiming that squalene "produces a more efficient metabolic process," "detoxifies the body," acts as an

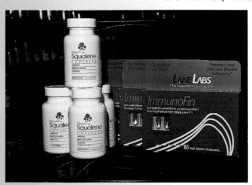

You can find squalene on health-food store shelves. Above photo taken at Huckleberry Farms on Nu'uanu Ave.

"antioxidant," and "boosts the immune system." Marketing slogans tell us that squalene "improves blood flow" in the coronary arteries, "prolongs blood coagulation," and "lowers cholesterol" in heart tissue. Any unpleasant side effects are due to massive extractions of toxins from the body, claim squalene's distributors. Ads even tout squaline as a fountain of youth that will keep you feeling young and improve your sexual appetite. So far, none of these claims have been supported by verifiable evidence. However, there may be health benefits to squalene, which contains some ingredients found in a typical daily vitamin supplement. According to 1999 research by Harold Newmark of the Rutgers University Laboratory for Cancer Research, the squalene in olive oil might reduce the risk of certain cancers (colon, breast, pancreas), but further studies are needed.

Olive oil is high in squalene.

As a side note, some interesting squalene shenanigans took place in the 1940s when European olive oil was scarce after WWII. Olive oil, it seems, contains a higher concentration of squalene (3.3 mg. per gram) than cheaper vegetable oils (0.1 mg. per gram in soya bean oil, and 0.3 mg. per gram in peanut oil). Some unscrupulous individuals took advantage of this fact by buying squalene—a by-product separated out during the extraction of vitamin A from shark-liver oil—from pharmaceutical companies. They mixed it with cheaper oils and sold the mixture as higher-priced olive oil, claiming that it included 20% olive oil, when, in fact, no olive oil was present. The ruse worked because, even though the mixture did not smell like olive oil, the Federal Food and Drug Administration (FDA) verified the presence of olive oil by testing for squalene concentration. The million-dollar fraud continued until an ex-FDA chemist noticed that squalene sales had skyrocketed. He informed the FDA, which investigated by marking pharmaceutical squalene with harmless and stable anthranilic acid and then testing various brands of olive oil for the acid, thus exposing the deception.

Shark Cartilage

A shark's backbone is made completely of cartilage.

In the late 1970s and early 1980s, the possibility that cartilage might contain anti-tumor properties fueled an independent line of cancer research. The amazing discovery of an anti-cancer protein compound was first reported after testing calf cartilage, but soon scientists were looking at cartilaginous fish such as sharks and rays as a potential source of the new compound. Since sharks have a low incidence of cancer and an entire skeleton made up of cartilage, the science world reasoned, they could serve as a ready source.

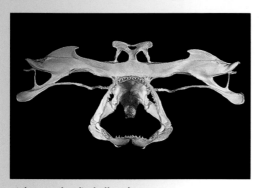

A hammerhead's skull and jaws may look like bone, but they're actually hardened cartilage.

Shark cartilage capsules have no proven health benefits.

Two fallacies invalidate this line of reasoning, however. Although only eight to ten cases of cancer in sharks and rays have been reported, the ocean is a big place and thousands of unreported cases might exist. Also, the anti-cancer protein compound had been isolated by treating cartilage with chemicals and producing a liquid extract. In the rush to market this new product as a cancer cure, the liquid-extract approach was abandoned, and whole cartilage was ground up and bound into pills or sold as dry powder, neither of which had been tested for effectiveness.

As a result of aggressive marketing, an estimated 50,000 Americans ingest some form of shark cartilage as part of their anti-cancer therapy or as the sole treatment. Few objective trials have been conducted. And because these products are marketed as dietary supplements, they do not come under the rigorous scrutiny of the Food and Drug Administration and are readily available in supermarkets and at health-food stores. A 1995-96 study by the Cancer Treatment Research Foundation found that powdered shark cartilage provided no benefits when it was used to treat advanced cancer patients. There was no sign of cancer regression, but some patients suffered from nausea, vomiting and constipation.

In the authors' opinion, it doesn't make sense to kill thousands of sharks and grind up the cartilage, then market the product as a food supplement without making any effort to identify an active ingredient. A more practical approach involves isolating a bioactive compound from the tissues of a few animals, identifying its structure, synthesizing the molecule, and demonstrating that the synthetic version is just as active as the natural version before touting its potential applications in human cancer therapy. Using this approach, it's possible to learn from these animals without wiping them out in the process.

Recent studies have concentrated on liquid cartilage extract as a potential cancer therapy, and clinical trials are now underway. Studies to date indicate that liquid cartilage extract did reduce tissue reaction when foreign substances were introduced into the arms of research subjects, however this is a long way from reducing or regressing cancer tumor growth. To be effective, the protein compound must pass through stomach acids without being broken down, be absorbed by the intestine in sufficient quantities, and then locate and neutralize the cancer cells.

On an ironic note, we may be able to supply our own anti-cancer treatment. Troponin I, a compound in human cartilage, has recently been identified and shows anti-cancer promise. It will be interesting to follow the trials of Troponin I and see if an already existing compound in the human body can lead to a cancer cure.

Squalamine

In pre-clinical tests, squalamine significantly reduced the growth of lung, ovarian, breast, prostate and brain tumors, and it is currently in Phase II clinical testing for non-small-cell lung cancer.

Discovered in the stomach lining of a spiny dogfish shark and recently synthesized, this steroidal antibiotic also destroys a wide variety of fungi and bacteria. In addition to small amounts of squalamine in the stomach, gills and intestine of the shark, larger concentrations are found in the liver and gallbladder, with the spleen and testes containing half as much.

Cornea Transplants

Once considered a potential source of cornea transplants for humans, shark corneas apparently proved ineffective. No research reports have been published in recent years.

Toxic Sharks

Because sharks are top predators and eat a variety of other animals, their muscles and internal organs are prime receptacles for toxins. Ciguatera, for example, is a toxin produced by dinoflagellates—tiny algae that are ingested by reef fish, which are subsequently eaten by predatory fish (i.e. sharks). Observations in the Marshall Islands found that the flesh of a gray reef shark, whitetip reef shark and blacktip shark (all found in Hawai'i) caused a slight ciguatera toxic reaction when consumed by a mongoose. However, no cases of ciguatera from these sharks have been reported in Hawai'i.

This unicorn fish and other reef fish may contain toxins such as ciguatera.

In humans, this toxin can cause tingling or numbness in the hands, diarrhea, confusion when sensing hot versus cold, and difficulty in breathing. Symptoms commonly persist for six weeks (sometimes longer) and can be reinitiated by eating seafood or drinking alcohol.

As environmental sentinels, sharks can warn us of ocean pollutants.

Another toxin, carchatoxin A and B, killed 50 people who ate the liver and muscle of a 220-pound bull shark *(Carcharhinus leucas)* in Madagascar. Five to ten hours after eating the shark (one that is commonly eaten in this area without adverse effects), the local hospital admitted 188 patients who complained of burning or stinging sensations in their lips or mouths and numbness in their arms and legs—neurological symptoms of toxic poisoning. Some of these patients lapsed into comas before dying.

In Greenland, although eating the dried meat of the Greenland shark is a common practice, eating the fresh meat of the same species made sled dogs sick and caused poisoning intoxication in humans. No pelagic (open ocean) sharks have been reported with carchatoxin, nor has it been reported in any sharks from Hawai'i.

Pollutants dumped into waterways that feed the ocean show up in the ocean's top predator. Many coastal sharks have elevated mercury concentrations, which increase with age as sharks take in more mercury, primarily through their diet. Sharks can also pass mercury directly to their offspring. One study revealed fetal sharks with mercury levels 8-60% as high as their mothers. In both Australia and the United States, many species of coastal sharks exceed the current standard of 0.5 mg of mercury per kg of muscle tissue. In Florida, for example, 12% of the sharks tested had concentrations greater than 1.5 mg of mercury. Even deep-sea sharks in certain geographic areas are prone to increased mercury concentrations, and these concentrations can be higher than in coastal sharks.

As these facts demonstrate, top predators such as sharks can serve as environmental sentinels—indicators of ecosystem quality and degradation.

Visitors can watch through underwater windows as a diver feeds rays in the Reef Tank at Sea Life Park.

CHAPTER 8

SHARKS AND RAYS IN AQUARIUMS

When we think of sharks, we often think of the movie *Jaws*. In 1980, when the Shark Encounter exhibit at Sea World of Florida first opened, the *Jaws* image of a monster with huge, razor-sharp teeth attacking without warning was so fearsome that parents were overheard reassuring their terrified children that the captured sharks' teeth had been removed (not true, of course). Because of that movie and other stories of man-eating sharks, many of us nurture a deep-seated fear of the ocean's top predator. But we're also curious about this often mysterious animal, and aquariums provide a unique opportunity to come face to face with sharks in a safe environment and to learn more about them.

One of the first shark exhibits in Hawai'i took place in the early 1900s at the annual Honolulu County Fair. Captain Bill Young, co-founder of Young Brothers, a prolific shark hunter and author of the book Shark! Shark! (Gotham House, Inc. 1933) harpooned and killed a large tiger shark. He packed the female shark in ice, along with 42 embryonic pups from her uterus, and displayed them at the fair, charging ten cents admission. By the end of the week, he had collected $1,500 "in a town where," he said, "Young Brothers hung sharks up on the wharf every other day or so in full view of all and sundry without charge."

Courtesy of Young Brothers.

Captain Bill Young (holding harpoon) and a tiger shark on the Honolulu wharf circa 1900.

Hired as the first manager of the Honolulu Aquarium, which opened in 1904 just 'Ewa (west) of the current Waikīkī Aquarium (1955), Captain Young tells of an eight-foot tiger shark that he kept in an outdoor tank set in the ground, making the facility the first aquarium in North America to exhibit a tiger shark. In 1976, the Waikīkī Aquarium followed in its predecessor's footsteps and became the first aquarium in North America to exhibit a blacktip reef shark.

Jack Randall

Viewers can see sharks such as this blacktip reef through plexiglass windows at Hawai'i's public aquariums.

Today in Hawai'i, close to one million people a year get up-close and personal with well-cared-for sharks and rays at three aquariums: Maui Ocean Center, Sea Life Park and the Waikīkī Aquarium; and even at some retail outlets and hotels such as Waikīkī's Pacific Beach Hotel, the Big Island's Mauna Lani Bay Hotel and Bungalows, and the Four Seasons Resort at Hualalai. Public education classes, underwater videos, exhibit graphics and exhibit narrations by experienced biologists help to bring about a new understanding and appreciation of both sharks and rays. The Waikīkī Aquarium, for example, periodically offers its immensely popular program, Sharks Overnight, in which children and their parents learn about sharks, make shark models out of surfboard foam, roll out their sleeping bags to spend the night near the shark tank, and then test their models the next morning in a racing tank.

Aquariums offer other experiences, too. Feeding times, when divers in the tank feed sharks and rays by hand, always draw an eager crowd. At Sea Life Park visitors can swim with rays in a shallow lagoon, hand-feed them in a specially designed touch pool, or take a walk on the wet-and-wild side—along the bottom of the reef tank wearing a breathing helmet while surrounded by streamlined sharks and bat-winged rays.

Watching sharks through a plexiglass window (or joining them in the tank) can be an exhilarating experience, but behind the scenes, caring for captive sharks and rays is a complex and often time-consuming process. We think of sharks as being extremely hardy and practically indestructible, but

Guests are invited to feed spotted eagle rays at the Four Seasons Resort, Hualalai on the Big Island.

Waikīkī Aquarium volunteers learn about sharks on a field trip to the Hawai'i Institute of Marine Biology.

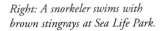

Right: A snorkeler swims with brown stingrays at Sea Life Park.

Children at the Waikīkī Aquarium's Sharks
Overnight program show off their shark models.

To monitor the health of large sharks, a hammock
comes in handy.

Measuring and health checks take only a few minutes.

Working with sharks can be dangerous.

in fact, they must be handled carefully. Transferring them from the ocean to the aquarium, for example, requires special tools. Smaller sharks are sometimes transported in a round container (so that they can keep swimming) equipped with an oxygen bottle and a regulator, which distributes the right amount of oxygen to the water. Larger sharks might be lifted out of the water using a specially designed stretcher or "shark brassiere," a kind of hammock with pockets in the sides to accommodate the shark's pectoral fins.

Aquarium exhibit tanks must be designed so that sharks have adequate room to maneuver, grow and reproduce. Visitors to aquariums often ask why there are no great whites or blue sharks on display, and the answer is simple. These and other open-ocean sharks are adapted for long periods of cruising or gliding when they must rest their swimming muscles. Gliding over long distances requires space not available in most aquariums.

All ages enjoy feeding the rays at Sea Life Park.

A few aquariums have attempted to display great white sharks. OceanWorld in Sydney, Australia, kept one in captivity for five days, but the shark kept bumping its head against the side of the tank and had to be released to keep it from hurting itself. Sea World of California displayed a great white shark for sixteen days; and Hawai'i Marineland in Kewalo Basin had a 1,600-pound, 13-foot-4-inch-long great white on view for two days, according to the March 9, 1961 issue of the *Honolulu Star-Bulletin*.

Unless aquarium biologists understand a shark's lifestyle, habitat, methods of reproduction, food, and other requirements, the shark might have difficulty adapting to aquarium life, could become weak or disoriented, and if not returned to the ocean in time, might die. Tiger sharks, known for being aggressive in the wild, appear almost timid in aquariums and must be fed at a solitary location away from other feeding sharks. Tigers also require more food than other sharks and will pay more attention to their feeders, often rolling their bodies slightly to get a better look at the human with the bucket of fish.

Below: In aquariums, sharks are more likely to eat colorful fish than their duller-looking tank-mates.

Overfed sharks in aquariums might actually look overweight compared to their ocean-going relatives who eat relatively little in relation to their body size. Because of this and because the needs of each species are different, knowledgeable handlers feed sharks and rays individually, using tongs, to make sure they receive the correct amount of food. At the Waikīkī Aquarium, each blacktip reef shark is fed two pounds of fish and squid a week, a diet that helps them maintain a trim and healthy sleekness.

How do handlers tell animals apart to determine which ones have eaten their ration and which have not? Like whales, sharks and rays are identified by color and spot patterns on their bodies, but aquariums can also mark pectoral fins with daubs of harmless silver nitrate. The patterns and locations of these markings act like natural skin identifiers.

From left to right: Small sharks are collected using nets, then transported to outer-island and Mainland aquariums in seawater-filled, oxygenated plastic bags.

Left: From the top of the Waikīkī Aquarium's shark tank, an aquarist feeds a carefully balanced diet of squid and fish to a blacktip reef shark. Right: A stingray at the Waikīkī Aquarium reaches for its food.

Even if the aquarium pumps natural seawater into its tanks, sharks and rays might succumb to vitamin and mineral deficiencies when out of their natural habitat. For this reason they are given vitamin and mineral supplements along with their usual diet of fish, squid and shrimp. Until aquarists find the proper dietary balance, two of the most common problems that crop up are lack of enough vitamin E—the result of eating frozen food—and enlargement of the thyroid gland (goiter), caused by low levels of iodide in the water or inadequate absorption of iodide in the animal's body. Administering supplements usually remedies both conditions.

Sometimes visitors to aquariums ask, "Why don't the sharks eat other fish in the tank?" Occasionally they do, but because they are well fed, they usually leave their tank companions alone. When sharks do eat aquarium fish, they seem to prefer yellow tangs or other colorful species, as opposed to the more drab-looking specimens. The moral here might be, 'when you swim with sharks, it doesn't pay to call attention to yourself.'

Aquarium biologists have discovered that both sharks and rays have the ability to learn certain behaviors—both wanted and unwanted. In one case, bottom-feeding rays were taught to take fish and squid from the end of an aquarist's pole. Sharks in the tank soon learned that they could steal dinner by biting the rays to make them drop their food. In another instance, sharks were conditioned to swim through a maze with a food reward at the end.

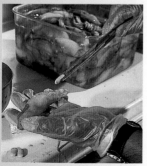

Vitamins are added to sharks' and rays' food at the Waikīkī Aquarium.

Aquariums, then, serve many purposes. In addition to public education and awareness, aquariums provide a venue where biologists can learn about shark and ray mating and feeding habits, reproduction, digestion, muscle function, social behavior, hydrodynamics and much more. Aquariums play a valuable role in helping us understand sharks and rays and their relationship to the ocean environment.

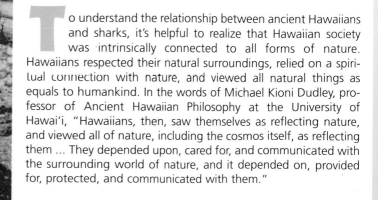

CHAPTER 9

HAWAIIANS AND SHARKS

The ama of a canoe (curved float supporting the outrigger beams) could be splintered by an angry shark.

This chapter has been compiled from the works of respected Hawaiian culture experts such as Mary Kawena Pukui, Samuel M. Kamakau, Martha Beckwith and others (see references in Bibliography). The authors wish to extend their profound gratitude for the understanding of Hawaiian culture that these works have provided and will continue to provide for future generations.

"The shark is a ravaging lion of the ocean whom none can tame. It is able to swallow a man down whole. If a man arouses its anger, it will show its rows of shining teeth with the sea washing between—and nothing can equal the terror which seizes a man when a shark chops to pieces the ama of his canoe and tosses him up and down in the sea. Holding the man securely between its upper and shorter lower law, it jerks him about on the surface of the sea."

— Samuel M. Kamakau, *The People of Old*

ho'omanō: [to behave as a shark, to act like a shark, to pursue women.]

pua ka wiliwili, nanahu ka manō.
[When] the wiliwili [tree] blooms, sharks bite
(said of a girl reaching maturity).

— Pukui & Elbert, *Hawaiian Dictionary*

o understand the relationship between ancient Hawaiians and sharks, it's helpful to realize that Hawaiian society was intrinsically connected to all forms of nature. Hawaiians respected their natural surroundings, relied on a spiritual connection with nature, and viewed all natural things as equals to humankind. In the words of Michael Kioni Dudley, professor of Ancient Hawaiian Philosophy at the University of Hawai'i, "Hawaiians, then, saw themselves as reflecting nature, and viewed all of nature, including the cosmos itself, as reflecting them ... They depended upon, cared for, and communicated with the surrounding world of nature, and it depended on, provided for, protected, and communicated with them."

Illustration by Jonah Okano.

It was not at all unusual for Hawaiians to conclude that the gods directing their lives communicated with them by appearing as natural forms such as rocks, insects, plants, waves and animals such as the shark. This belief invited the natural world to engage in an intimate relationship with the spiritual world.

Na Akua Manō (Shark Gods)

At the top of the hierarchy of Hawaiian spirits were the akua. According to Pukui, these were "distant, awesome deities, concerned with the mighty forces of land and sea, storm and calm, light of day and dark of night." In this revered group were the four major gods—Kū, Kāne, Kanaloa and Lono—as well as a host of lesser gods such as the volcano goddess Pele and her elder

An oceanside heiau: The spiritual and temporal worlds were one to ancient Hawaiians.

In ancient Hawai'i, gods controlled the mighty forces of land and sea.

brother, Kamohoali'i, who could transform himself into a shark and who was referred to as the king of sharks. It was in the form of a shark that he led his sister from their ancestral home to Hawai'i. Kamohoali'i's home is on a cliff overlooking the Halema'uma'u Crater at Kīlauea on the Big Island. This spot was considered so sacred that not even Pele dared to blow smoke across it. When Kamohoali'i takes human form, he appears without his loincloth—a privilege reserved for gods.

Other shark gods (akua manō) included Kuhaimoana, whose mouth was rumored to be as large as a grass house; Kauhuhu, the fierce king shark of Maui who lives in a cave in Kīpahulu and has a second home (guarded by mo'o deities) called Eel Cave on the windward side of Moloka'i; and Ka'ahupāhau and her brother Kahiuka (also called the Smiting Tail)—both reputed to have been born of human parents and to have changed into sharks—who lived in a cave at the entrance to Pearl Harbor and protected the people of 'Ewa from man-eating sharks.

When the new dry dock collapsed at Pearl Harbor in 1914, says Beckwith, many people believed that the shark guardians of the basin were still active. Historian Laura Green writes: "Today a floating dock is employed. Engineers say that there seem to be tremors of the earth at this point which prevent any structure from resting upon the bottom, but Hawaiians believe that 'the Smiting Tail' still guards the blue lagoon at Pearl Harbor." His shark sister is remembered in a Hawaiian proverb:

Ho'ahewa na niuhi ia Ka'ahupāhau

The man-eating sharks blamed Ka'ahupāhau
(Evil-doers blame the person who safeguards the rights of others.)

A bigeye thresher shark. Does 'the Smiting Tail' still guard the blue lagoon at Pearl Harbor?

Like the brother and sister above, these shark gods are often worshipped as protectors of people living in a particular district. A story about Kauhuhu, the terrible king shark god of Maui and Moloka'i, tells of a kahuna whose sons are killed by the chief's henchmen because the boys are caught playing the sacred temple drum at the heiau. The kahuna appeals to Kauhuhu for revenge, giving the shark god a black pig as a gift. At first Kauhuhu is angry that a mortal has entered his sea cave, but he listens to the man's plea and several months later the chief and all his followers are devoured by sharks when a storm sweeps them into the sea.

Kamakau tells us that at one time, O'ahu was protected by the shark gods Kanehunamoku and Pele's brother, Kamohoali'i, who decreed that no malihini (newcomer) shark who attempted to bite people in O'ahu waters would escape with his life. This edict was well known, and "only in recent times have sharks been known to bite people in O'ahu waters or to have devoured them," says Kamakau. "It was not so in old times."

There was one O'ahu shark who did bite in the old days—a shark with one tooth who nipped like a crab. Common wisdom at the time said that if a man was bitten by a shark that left a single toothmark, it was a warning that an enemy of the sea was approaching and that chiefs and commoners alike should make their way to shore.

'Aumakua (Ancestor God)

Sharks were also regarded as 'aumākua, ancestral deities. In her book, *Nana I Ke Kumu (Look to the Source)*, native Hawaiian historian Mary Kawena Pukui describes the 'aumākua.

> *"They are forever god-spirits, possessing the strange and awesome powers of gods. Yet they are forever our relatives, having for us the loving concern a mother feels for her infant, or a grandfather for his first-born grandson. As gods and relatives in one, they give us strength when we are weak, warning when danger threatens, guidance in our bewilderment, inspiration in our arts. They are equally our judges, hearing our words and watching our actions, reprimanding us for error, and punishing us for blatant offense. For these are our godly ancestors. These are our spiritual parents. These are our 'aumākua."*

Some 'aumākua were invisible spirits and others could inhabit inanimate forms such as a rock, or living creatures such as a shark. An ancestor could possess a particular shark in two ways, one of which was the deification ritual, kākū'ai, in which the family took the departed relative, wrapped in a distinctive tapa cloth, to the keeper of a shark deity. He, in turn, would place the body (or bundle of bones) under the fin of

Blacktip reef sharks like these were often turned into 'amākua for family protection.

Shark ʻaumakua herding fish into a fisherman's net. Illustration by Jonah Okano.

a shark that was resting in a cove. After a few days, the bundle became another shark, marked with the color and design of its wrapping—reddish, for example, if the tapa was red and white, or striped if it was a moelua tapa. This designation, along with personal markings such as a tattoo, enabled the family to recognize their own after he or she became a shark. The procedure is described by Pukui as follows:

"The kahu manō [shark caretaker] took ʻawa [intoxicating drink] at dawn and dusk for two or three days, until he saw clearly that the body had definitely assumed the form of a shark, and had changed into a little shark, with recognizable marks (of the deceased) on the cheeks or sides, like a tattoo or an earring mark. After two or three days more, when the kahu manō saw the strengthening of this new shark ... he sent for the relatives who had brought the body ... and when the relatives came they would see with their own eyes that it (the deceased) had become a shark, with all the signs by which they could not fail to recognize the loved one in a deep ocean. If the relatives should go bathing or fishing in the sea, it would come around and they would all recognize the markings of their own shark."

In 1823, Englishman William Ellis described a similar event, also thought to represent the kākūʻai:

"The fisherman sometimes wrapped their dead in red native cloth, and threw them into the sea, to be devoured by the sharks. Under the influence of a belief in the transmigration of souls, they supposed the spirit of the departed would animate the shark by which the body was devoured."

An ʻaumakua could also be born of a human mother and an akua manō (shark god) father who visited as a dream lover, as in the following event told to Martha Beckwith:

"It is related that a girl of thirteen years of age ... dreamed that a lover appeared to her out of the ocean. Every morning when she told her parents this dream her father thought she had allowed someone liberties and wanted to conceal it, so he kept her carefully guarded. The dreams however continued. After a time the girl gave birth to a shark. Her parents recognized this as the offspring of an akua manō called Kealiʻikaua O Kau, a cousin of Pele [the volcano goddess], and did not hold her responsible.

The young mother took the baby, wrapped it in green pakaiea (a coarse seaweed) and cast it into the sea. The young shark was always recognizable by its green coat, and became an ʻaumakua of that particular family."

Why would families want to turn their loved ones into shark 'aumākua? According to Kamakau,

> "Sometimes [during a shark attack] the body was bitten in two, and the head and trunk alone mauled about. It was because of such terrifying occurrences that people transfigured their beloved into sharks." And "because [guardian akua and 'aumākua] sharks save men in times of peril, protect them when other sharks try to devour them and are useful in other ways in saving lives at sea and on the deep ocean, some people were made into shark 'aumākua, or guardian gods." (Other reports tell of shark 'aumākua leading people to safety when their boats overturned or sank, and even carrying them to shore. It was said in ancient Hawai'i that members of a family with a shark 'aumakua could never be drowned.)

Also, perhaps, because, says Beckwith, a shark 'aumakua would drive fish into a fisherman's net in return for the first catch. And, says Pukui, if asked to bring a specific fish, the shark 'aumakua honored the request. Those with shark 'aumākua always returned home with full nets.

In each generation, one family member was chosen to become the shark 'aumakua's kahu, or keeper, who respectfully offered prayer, food and 'awa to the 'aumakua so it would continue to help the family. Without respect, the 'aumakua might punish or lose interest in the family and be unavailable in times of need.

Shark skin, especially the section covering the belly, was stretched over the heads of drums.

There were evil shark 'aumākua, too; deified ancestors turned bad. Some even attacked the kahu who had transfigured and deified them. Others performed evil deeds for their kahu, who might be a sorcerer. One story tells of a pretty girl on the Big Island of Hawai'i who arouses the jealousy of a neighboring family. When they give offerings to their shark 'aumakua to destroy her, she is carried away by a wave and eaten by a shark. Her mother, however, goes to a sorcerer who restores the girl through the birth of another child, and, in retribution, members of the other family become sick and die a miserable death.

On the whole, though, a family's relationship to its shark 'aumakua was a friendly and intimate one. Such a relationship enabled a family to enter the ocean without fear.

Rough shark skin wrapped around a wooden handle made an ideal rasp for wood sanding.

Manō (Shark)

Although the name for sharks in general is manō, the ancient Hawaiian language included many words describing different sharks. Names such as manō hi'ukā (smiting tail [thresher shark]), manō laukāhi'u (long-tailed), manō 'ula (red), manō pā'ele (black smudged [perhaps referring to the blacktip reef shark]), manō lelewa'a (canoe leaping), and manō pahāha (thick necked) might

Above—left: Manō kihikihi (hammerhead shark) meat was salted, dried and cooked when needed; right: Manō lālākea (whitetip reef shark) was a staple of the early Hawaiians' diet.

A shark tooth hand weapon with sennet grip.

Courtesy of the Waikiki Aquarium.

Great white (foreground) and tiger shark teeth were used to make weapons of war.

indicate different shark species or unique markings or behaviors of individual sharks. Some Hawaiian names are known to refer to certain species. Manō kihikihi (hammerhead) and manō lālākea (whitetip reef), for example, were the two most common edible sharks. Their meat was cut into strips, salted and dried, then cooked as needed by those families permitted to eat shark meat.

In addition to being a source of food, sharks had other uses. Thin but immensely tough and resilient, shark skin was stretched over the heads of large wooden drums. Its rough surface served as sandpaper for polishing bowls, and, wrapped around a wooden handle, as a rasp for other fine woodworking. Shark teeth, especially those of the tiger and great white, were made into brass-knuckle-style hand weapons, and lashed to war clubs, or mounted on wooden handles for use as knives or awls. Teeth were even affixed to ceremonial objects. One of the few surviving Hawaiian feather gods at Bishop Museum displays a mouth rimmed with sharks' teeth.

Fishing for Sharks

One shark in particular, the niuhi (some accounts describe this shark as a tiger, others as a great white), represented bravery, daring, strength, benevolence, protection and rescue. Since the niuhi was a symbol of the high chief who embodied all the above attributes, commoners could not fish for the great shark, nor were women allowed to eat its flesh. Niuhi fishing (called kūmanō, or shark roping) was more a demonstration or test of skill and courage than a quest for food. It was considered a sport for the ali'i since only the bravery of the ali'i could match that of the shark.

Once caught, all parts of the niuhi's body, including the bones, were used, as all were supposed to confer unflinching bravery on the possessor. Pukui tells us that "before [King] Kamehameha was born, his mother craved the eye of the fierce niuhi [which she was given to eat]. Because of this, even before he was born, people knew Kamehameha would grow up to be a ferocious fighter."

Members of the niuhi fishing expedition often used decomposed pig meat or even human flesh (the chiefs would have men killed secretly, says Kamakau)—sometimes laced with 'awa and mixed with pebbles and broken kukui nut shells—as chum to attract the shark. When the shark appeared, it was fed meat until it lost its fear of the canoe and swam in close. Then one of the bravest men slipped a noose over its head, and it was killed by the chief with a sharp weapon. As an alternative to killing the shark outright, the noose was secured to the canoe and the shark allowed to tire itself out (giving those in the canoe a wild ride) before a second noose was slipped over the tail and the shark pulled backwards in the water until it drowned. It was understood that the actual captor—the one who slipped the noose over the niuhi's head—would, from then on, be victorious in any endeavor.

Shark noosing. Illustration by Jonah Okano.

Shark fishing using a noose was also reported from the Trobriand Islands in the Solomon Sea. The noose, made of pandanus-root fiber, was threaded through the middle of a six-foot-long, hibiscus-wood float that looked like a two-bladed aircraft propeller. Sharks were called using a cane hoop threaded with twenty or so hard coconut shells, which could be rattled in the water. The next step was enticing the shark to swim through the noose with a fish lure, then the rope was pulled tight across its gills.

Other reports indicate that, after eating meat soaked in 'awa, the stupefied and roped niuhi followed the canoe, a willing prisoner, until it was stranded and killed in shallow water. Sometimes niuhi were caught on large baited hooks attached to handlines. In any case, niuhi fishing was not considered a sport for the timid.

Sennet lashing holds sections of a canoe together.

The smaller and less-aggressive food sharks, hammerhead and whitetip reef, could be found closer to shore and were not considered as dangerous as the niuhi. Larger sharks were caught on hooks up to 12-inches long, usually carved of hardwoods and tipped with sharp bone points. The Bishop Museum houses two rare shark hooks carved completely of bone.

A fisherman could also tame a young shark by petting its head until it was used to being touched and then, one day, slip a noose around the animal—being careful to keep his palms turned away, says Kamakau, "lest it see their whiteness (white palms might resemble a silvery fish) and turn and bite them." The fisherman would then press down on the shark's head with his foot.

Shark fishing hooks were often made of wood with bone tips.

John Naughton

Tiger shark fishing today—
no longer a sport of kings.

According to Kamakau writing in the 1870s, there were also other shark-fishing methods: "If the fishermen were afraid, a snare made of crossed sticks of wauke noosed the shark," or "sharks were seized with the hands. Oʻahu was a land famous for just seizing sharks; porpoises; rays; and other fishes."

To the children, says Kamakau, "the shark was a horse to be bridled, its fin serving as a pommel of an Italian saddle. I have seen a man skilled in steering sharks ride a shark like a horse, turning it this way and that as it carried him to land—where he killed it."

Not much information about rays is available in Hawaiian literature. The brown stingray and eagle ray (also known as the spotted stingray) are referred to as hīhīmanu (bird-like) and lupe (kite-shaped), but the names seem to have been interchangeable. Pukui believes neither were eaten by Hawaiians of old, but were occasionally consumed by Hawaiians of her day, who baked them in an imu, salted and wrapped in ti leaves. Sometimes they were simply salted and dried into tough, hard strips. Pukui also tells us that rays were seen in the deep water off the Nā Pali coast of Kauaʻi, where they came close to shore during periods of high surf. This behavior, during a calm spell, was considered an indication that rough seas could be expected in a few hours. Rays were also common in Kāneʻohe Bay in midsummer, flipping their wings along the surface of the water.

It's interesting to note that even though the ancient Hawaiians had respect for animals, and even revered certain ones as gods, they were, at the same time, willing to eat them (those who had shark ʻaumākua did not eat shark meat, nor did they use tools, weapons or images made with shark teeth or skin; however, others did). Hawaiians were a practical people, and animals were considered food. But from all accounts, early Hawaiians did not take the ocean's bounty for granted, nor did they waste it. When a shark was caught, offerings of thanks were made to the appropriate akua and/or ʻaumakua for guiding the fishermen and giving them bravery and strength. And, with the exception of niuhi flesh, which was considered too potent for regular human consumption, the shark's meat was eaten and the skin and teeth used for tools and weapons.

Rays leaping in Kāneʻohe Bay.
Illustration by Ruth Cabanting.

Shark Attacks

The first documented observation of a shark attack in Hawaiian waters came from Edgar's journal during one of Captain Cook's expeditions. The incident, logged on December 23, 1778 off the Hilo coast of the Big Island of Hawai'i, reads as follows:

"....saw three very large Sharks about, the Men & Women Swimming to and from the ship at the same time About 1/2 past 11 a large shark attackd A man in the water, as Soon as he saw him Opening his Mouth & turning on his Side to lay hold of his Thigh he struck him on the Head with His Hand. Immediately the shark swam off. the Man who was rather Elderly seem'd very much alarm'd for a little time altho many Indians saw this and Made a Hallowing at the time, they do not seem to fear them as they Kept swimming abt as if there had been None seen."

In spite of guardian 'aumākua, and the fact that fishermen were intimately familiar with a shark's habitat, some ancient Hawaiians were attacked and maimed or killed by sharks. Kamakau reports one such story:

"In the country districts of Maui I have often seen persons who had been maimed by a shark—a foot cut off, a hand cut short, one side, or both, of the buttocks gone, the back badly scarred, the face marred, the eye and cheek torn away, and so forth." He met one woman in Lahaina in 1845 whose body was *"cut and ridged back and front from her head to her feet"* when she was *"nearly engulfed by a shark....(she) had dived to set a fish trap, and after making it fast in the current, she returned to the coral head where her companion was chewing bait, took the bait, and dived again to put it into the trap.....she felt the sea warm about her feet and herself being gulped down. Her whole body was inside the mouth of a shark when....she saw an opening between the rows of sharp teeth and struggled out, with the help of a little shark who splashed and drove the other away. She was badly torn, and lay on the rock and fainted dead away, but she was still living."*

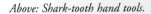

Courtesy of the Waikiki Aquarium.

Above: Shark-tooth hand tools.

Inset—left: Oily kukui nut torches once provided illumination for night fishing.

Below: Niuhi or manō kanaka (shark man)? Either way, the great white is a ferocious opponent.

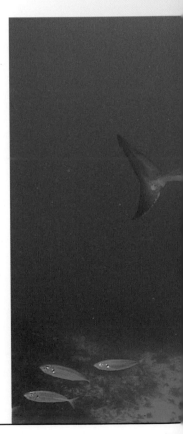

Small sharks (hand held) are among the fish caught at a hukilau.

Courtesy of the Hawai'i State Archives.

Ian Gordon

Although there were no documented organized shark hunts following an attack, there may indeed have been retribution, as illustrated in the many stories of manō kanaka or shark men.

These legendary shark men, although having different names and living in different places in the Hawaiian Islands, had a lot in common. They could change at will from human form to shark form, would issue a shark warning to passers-by going to the sea, and could be identified by the mark of a shark's open mouth on their backs (always kept covered by a cape of some sort). Once identified, shark-men were killed and the shark attacks subsided. One such story follows:

> The shark man Iwahaonou lived in the Pu'uanahulu and Pu'uwa'awa'a region of Kona on the Big Island. He was usually in his garden hoeing sweet potatoes or watering cane when the women and children of his district passed by on their way to the ocean, and he would always ask if they were going to the beach, then warn them about the man-eating shark, saying "Remember it is early, and the shark hasn't eaten his breakfast yet. Be sure you don't pick any sugar cane on your way, either, because sugar cane belongs to Hui, the shark, and is kapu."

> The warning was never heeded as the women and children loved to chew on the cane and suck its sweet juice on their way to fish for crabs and 'opihi, and this was the signal for Iwahaonou to take a shorter route to the beach, turn into Hui, the ferocious shark, and devour one or two of the luckless wanderers.

> Then one day, Moemoe, the prophet of Pele, arrived at the beach where the men often played checkers. Iwahaonou was one of the players that day and Moemoe instantly recognized him as a kupua (shark man). Iwahaonou, too, was disturbed by Moemoe's presence, and the two men challenged each other to a fight, with Iwahaonou trying to lure Moemoe into the ocean before the conflict. Unsuccessful, Iwahaonou went into the

ocean alone, supposedly to bathe, while Moemoe warned the others about the shark man. At first they didn't believe him, but changed their minds when they heard their wives and children screaming.

When Iwahaonou returned, the men tore off his dirty kīhei to find a snapping shark's mouth in the middle of his back, and threw him onto the red and glowing rocks of the imu, which dried him to dust. From then on the people of the district were safe to bathe and fish in the warm waters of the Kona sea.

It appears that after an attack or series of attacks without provocation, only the responsible shark was singled out and killed. In this way, Hawaiians did not disturb the balance of life in the ocean.

Early Hawaiians, then, believed that some sharks were good and some were bad. Some sharks attacked people, and some, especially 'aumākua, rescued their descendants, even from other sharks. Sharks could be vengeful, angry creatures or helpful allies. When the first Hawaiians sailed here from Tahiti, says Kamakau, "They were guided over the desolate wastes like beloved children by a single great guide, the shark named Kalahiki."

This two-pronged association—bravery, strength and protection versus fright, danger and death—existed during the time of Mary Kawena Pukui, Samuel Kamakau and others whose writings are a window into the world of ancient Hawai'i. Today, many of the old beliefs, long buried, are resurfacing and returning Hawaiians to their cultural roots. The following story, related by a Big Island resident whose family 'aumakua on his mother's side is the shark, exemplifies one of those beliefs.

The story begins the evening before a celebration at Pu'ukoholā (Hill of the Whale) heiau (temple) near Kawaihae Harbor in 1991. The event was planned as a rededication of the temple and a clearing away of resentments between family descendants of Kamehameha I and his cousin and rival Keoua, who was killed by Kamehameha's warriors and offered as a sacrifice to the war god Kuka'ilimoku when this temple was first built and dedicated.

Ceremonial rites at a shark heiau. Illustration by Ruth Cabanting.

"One of my cousins went down for the evening [ritual] cleansing in the ocean before the big celebration the following day. Right below the heiau is a shark heiau. it was built underwater (the water comes up to your waist and deeper) to feed the shark god. While they were doing the cleansing, my cousin, who was watching from the shore, saw a big shark—ten feet or bigger—come in. It stayed about 100 feet away from them and didn't move, just idled and watched. There are sharks, whitetips, down there every day circling, but this one didn't move. After the cleansing and the prayer, the shark left. The old kupuna said, 'oh, (the shark god) came to watch.' They thought it was a good sign."

Cynthia Vanderlip

Shark Proverbs

From *'Olelo No'eau,* a book compiled by Mary Pukui, the following sampling of proverbs and sayings indicates the importance of sharks in Hawaiian culture:

Pau Pele, pau manō.

[May I be] devoured by Pele, [may I be] devoured by a shark.

An oath meaning "If I fail...." It was believed that if such an oath were not kept, the one who spoke it would die by fire or be eaten by a shark.

He manō holo 'āina ke ali'i.

The chief is a shark that travels on land.

The chief, like a shark, is not to be tampered with. [It may also mean that a chief devours the wealth of the land as ravenously as a shark devours the fishes of the sea.]

Uliuli kai holo ka manō.

Where the sea is dark, sharks swim.

Sharks are found in the deep sea. Also applied to men out seeking the society of the opposite sex.

Ke pau ka moa, kākā i ka nuku; ke pau ka 'iole, ahu kūkae; ke pau ka manō, lana i ke kai.

When a chicken finishes [eating] he cleans his beak; when a rat finishes, he leaves a heap of excreta; when a shark finishes, he rises to the surface of the sea.

A description of the table manners of people. Some are clean like the chicken; others are unclean and careless like the rat; and still others, like the shark, loll around without offering to help.

CHAPTER 10

FISHERIES

John Naughton

Thresher sharks are still eaten today in Hawai'i.

In the year 1900, O'ahu's fishing fleet caught 1,533 sharks weighing 10,300 pounds and sold them for $686 at Honolulu fish markets. That same year, vendors also peddled 60 stingrays (weighing 1,790 pounds) for the tidy sum of $790.

Although the above numbers seem relatively small, at the time they were not much smaller than Hawai'i's tuna fishery, today a $35-million operation, but which, at the turn of the century, brought in a mere $2,014.

For Island residents, fisheries provide an important source of food. Sustaining those fisheries, though, is not an easy task because ocean dynamics are not well understood. Management of shark and ray fisheries poses even more of a problem because these highly migratory species move around with no regard to countries' marine territorial boundaries. Also, unlike tuna and other sought-after food fish, sharks and rays grow slowly, mature to reproductive age later in life, and produce relatively few offspring, making overfishing an eventual certainty in many cases.

Early Hawaiians operated a limited but well-maintained shark fishery (according to Mary Pukui, they ate no rays until her time [late 1800s]). Sharks were caught in shallow coastal waters by using gill nets and purse seines (a large net, with sinkers on one edge and floats on the other; it hangs vertically in the water until it is dragged to shore or until the ends are pulled together, enclosing the catch; used at a hukilau), by noosing the shark around its gills, or by lassoing the shark's tail and pulling it backwards until it drowned.

Above: Hilo fishermen pull in a net to check their catch, circa 1900.

Left–inset: Hawaiian with net.

Below: Noosing a tiger shark today is not the dangerous sport it was in old Hawai'i.

Larger, offshore sharks could cause considerable damage by ripping through a painstakingly crafted net. To attract and trap these sharks, fishermen in canoes first suspended a basket filled with baked liver and other meat (decomposed pig meat and occasionally human flesh [Kamakau, 1976 p. 87]) under a canoe, then snared the dangerous animals on large hooks carved from hardwoods and tipped with sharp bone points. A piece of bone lashed to the upper part of the wooden hook often served as a securing end, and some hooks were carved completely of bone.

Following the scent of decomposed meat, the ferocious niuhi (either a tiger or great white; reports describe both) usually arrived at the canoes' location in three or four days' time. There it gorged on 'awa-laced meat and, when stupefied, was noosed around its gills and tied to a canoe for the trip back to shore. (for further details about the royal sport of niuhi fishing, see **Chapter 9: Hawaiians and Sharks**.)

Opah on ice at the fish auction.

Above: Buyers from fish markets, restaurants and hotels bid on mahimahi and 'ahi at the Honolulu fish auction.

Courtesy of the Waikiki Aquarium.

Close up of a shark fishing hook's bone tip and sennet lashing.

Early Hawaiians considered hammerhead and whitetip reef the most edible sharks. Once the skin was removed, the meat was cut into strips and salted or dried for later consumption. Sometimes the skin was left on, the meat salted overnight and either broiled or cooked in an imu, then eaten the next day. The flesh of a shark was never eaten raw, unlike that of other fish.

In 1859 a small fishery that included sharks was started in the Northwestern Hawaiian Islands. According to *Commercial Fisheries of the Hawaiian Islands,* published in 1902 and written by John N. Cobb, the Gambia, a three-masted sailing ship, returned from its three-and-a-half-month fishing trip with "a quantity of sharks' fins and (liver) oil." The fishery proved unsuccessful, however, as several ships ran aground. Cobb also reports that very little shark fishing took place in the late 1800s due to "lack of profitable markets for the products obtained."

Hawai'i's primary fisheries in 1900 concentrated on akule (bigeye scad) (224,033 fish weighing 839,328 lbs), mullet (100,571 fish/ 721,661 lbs), and flyingfish (252,915 fish / 573,082 lbs). As mentioned earlier, 'ahi (tuna) (a total of 250 lbs) made up a very small part of the catch. The majority of sharks and rays captured at this time were hooked on fishing lines, while others found themselves caught in bag or gill nets.

The Hawai'i longline fishery began in 1917 with techniques copied from Japanese longline fisheries, and wooden sampan-style bait-boats used in pole-and-line skipjack tuna operations. By 1950, boats were 40 to 63 feet long and carried twelve tons of ice to chill

Left: On the Havana's wooden sluice, bait and hooks are attached to fishing line as it is played out behind the moving boat. In port, rope bundles (baskets) sit coiled and ready for the next trip.

Right: Fishing line-marker buoys at the ready on Havana's deck.

Tom Webster's schooner Havana.

Havana's fishermen must be able to tie seaworthy knots during a three- or four-week fishing trip.

an average catch of three tons landed during a ten-day fishing trip. An old-style longline segment was called a basket and consisted of a rope stored in a bamboo container (the basket). Connected to each other, these ropes formed one continuous line.

With the exception of Tom Webster's classic Pacific Northwest halibut schooner *Havana*, (boats of this type were built between 1910 and 1929), none of Honolulu's fishing boats use baskets today. Since 1985, Hawai'i's modern longline fleet has reeled out a continuous main line of nylon monofilament dotted with snap-on monofilament branch lines. Also, with the advent of larger boats, fishing fleets gained the freedom to explore more distant fishing grounds and, in the early 1990s, to follow schools of swordfish in response to a rapidly expanding swordfish market. In 1991, leaving the nearshore fishing grounds to local anglers and small-boat fishing operations, the average longliner hauled in its catch more than 50 nautical miles from the main Hawaiian Islands. Just ten years later, the modern Hawai'i longline boat stretches 65 to 90 feet in length and can operate 2,000 miles from Honolulu.

Honolulu's fishing boats in port.

Inevitably, with the expansion of the longline fishery, a larger number of sharks have been caught. Hawaiian longline records for 1991 report catches totaling 71,183 sharks (65,481 blue sharks) primarily as bycatch, along with 68,243 'ahi (tuna), 66,289 swordfish, 39,525 mahimahi (dolphinfish), and other assorted pelagic fish. Makos and threshers are the only sharks regularly sold for their meat, and you'll find them on ice, awaiting bidders at the early-morning Honolulu fish auction. The following table indicates the numbers of blue, mako and thresher sharks caught from 1991 to 1999.

HAWAI'I-BASED LONGLINE FISHERY TOTALS FOR BLUE, MAKO AND THRESHER SHARKS

Southwest Fisheries Science Center
National Marine Fisheries Service

YEAR	BLUE	MAKO	THRESHER	TOTAL
1991	65,481	1,335	1,236	68,052
1992	89,292	1,008	1,608	91,908
1993	150,216	1,314	853	152,465
1994	110,187	1,075	1,460	112,722
1995	94,881	1,793	1,805	98,479
1996	96,214	1,146	1,887	99,247
1997	80,008	1,169	2,334	83,511
1998	91,228	1,384	3,842	96,454
1999	78,106	1,625	3,716	83,447
Total				886,283

A carpet keeps this mako shark and all hands from sliding on slippery decks.

Andrew Vatter, NMFS-PIAO

Shark logs in a ship's hold.

John Buchanan, NMFS-PIAO

Prize catch—a mako shark.

Worldwide, the catch of sharks, rays and skates (similar to rays, but none are found in Hawai'i) reached 6.4 million metric tons in the decade 1982 to 1991. In 1991 alone, this worldwide fishery reported an estimated catch of 700,000 metric tons (as a comparison, the 1991 Hawaiian Islands longline fishery landed 130 metric tons of sharks). These numbers are understated because many countries do not report their totals to the Food and Agriculture Organization (FAO) of the United Nations. For many small nations, shark meat, served either fresh or salted and dried, is an important source of food. But out of the 700,000 metric tons, only 66,847 metric tons, or about ten percent, ended up on the dinner table. An additional 36 metric tons was mined for its liver oil, and 240 metric tons—about thirty-four percent of the catch—was either discarded, or, in the case of sharks, finned and then discarded.

Right (next page):
A shark puts up
a fierce fight.

Courtesy of NMFS/FAO

Dried shark fins.

Shark Finning

To early Hawaiians, shark finning (cutting off a shark's fins and throwing the carcass back into the sea) was unheard of. Hawaiians made good use of all parts of the sharks they caught and believed that to throw away any part would be wasteful. During the mid-1800s, the small-scale practice of shark finning temporarily expanded with reports of an abundant supply of sharks in the Northwestern Hawaiian Islands. Then, as now, fins were dried and shipped to China and San Francisco as the key ingredient in shark-fin soup (which currently ranges in price from $114 to $190 a bowl, depending on availability and species of shark).

Hawai'i's longline fishery expressed very little interest in finning until 1991 when fins from 1,082 sharks brought higher-than-usual prices. By 1998, fins were removed from sixty percent (60,083 sharks) of the total sharks captured by Hawai'i's longline fishery. Blue sharks represented just over ninety-two percent (55,410 sharks) of those finned, yet the reportedly lower-quality blue shark fins command up to $26 per pound, as opposed to approximately $50 per pound for the fins of other shark species.

According to the United Nations' FAO catch reports, world exports of dried shark fins totaled 43,732 metric tons worth $600 million during the decade 1982 to 1991. To produce that many fins, it would take an estimated 20 million sharks—many more than the 6.4 million sharks, rays and skates reported. The true number probably lies somewhere between those figures.

Hong Kong and Singapore, as the world's largest shark-fin traders, account for 84 percent of the total volume of fins bought and sold. Also taking part in this lucrative trade, the United States imported 241 metric tons of shark fins in 1991—about six percent of the total reported shark-fin import trade. Although the U.S. did not record shark-fin exports in 1991, Hong Kong customs records for that year indicate that the U.S. was that country's fourth largest supplier of dried or salted shark fins, with shipments of 413 metric tons.

WILD ENCOUNTERS

Like Father, Like Son

It was five o'clock on a Friday afternoon in August during the ulua-only fishing tournament sponsored by the Waipouli Variety Store when I parked my 'okole on the lounge chair under a makeshift plastic shelter. It always rains in Hanalei and I wanted to be prepared. My lines were out so I popped open a can of ice cold soda, kinda' hoping nothing would bite for at least fifteen minutes.

Wrong! First the bell started ringing then the sound was all ratchet. My 30-year-old Fenwick pole was bent over, line screaming out from the Penn Senator 4-0. I asked myself, "Could this be THE fish?" As I removed the bell and took hold of the rod, I could feel the power of whatever was on the other end. Alas, it was not a typical ulua-type fight but more of a steady relentless power pull. Shark or stingray, I guessed. Either was a nuisance. This fishing area has a history of shark and stingray hookups. Sometime back one of my reels got stripped, and I was determined not to let that happen again. For about five minutes I pumped that stubborn animal, and then the line went slack—cut. I retrieved most of the line and was pretty sure it was a good-sized shark because the roughness at the broken end of the line was probably rubbing against the rough texture of the shark's skin. Fine with me and aloha to that shark. I rigged up a new leader system and went back to fishing.

Two days later, while I was unloading my truck at home, my son arrived. He had entered the same tournament, but he and his friend fished at a place called Stone Crusher in the Kīlauea area, out on the rocky point from the reservoir. It was more of a slide bait area. Anyway, he came up to me and said, "I bet you had lose one shark." "Yeh," I said, "One shark cut my line Friday afternoon. How you know? Somebody see and tell you?" He held out his hand and there was my leader system, hook, swivel, crimp, etc.

Glenn and Randall Takenaka.

Everyone has his own unique leader style and he knew mine. He said it was Saturday night when he had a tremendous strike, but when he brought it up, it was this seven-foot tiger shark. On close inspection, he saw my hook leader hanging out of the shark's mouth, so he got it out with pliers and couldn't wait to tell me. He also wanted to brag that while I lost it, he was able to land it. "Of course," I told him. "The shark was all tired out after its battle with me."

According to the scale on a map of Kaua'i, it was seven miles from where I lost the shark to where my son brought it up. We have caught sharks before with hooks and leaders dangling out of their mouths, but what are the odds of two members of the same family catching the same shark seven miles and 24 hours apart? To me this was a truly remarkable incident, and that's my shark story.

Submitted by Glenn Takenaka

Courtesy of Dale Sarver.

Anchors Away

It all started early Saturday morning when I took our 16-foot *Ali'i Kai* south from Honokohau Harbor along Ono Alley going south. I ran the 50-fathom line all the way down to Cook Monument without seeing a single fish. No birds, no bait, no strikes, no fish. Not such a great day for ono.

There's a spot south of Kealakekua Bay, about 60 feet deep, where there is a lot of coral and huge peacock bass, so I thought I would take a break and get in some diving. Just as I was figuring out where to put down the anchor, I saw a huge manta ray—

I'd guess it was about 10 feet across—swim right under the boat. Excited about the possibility of seeing this magnificent creature up close while diving, I dropped the anchor in 73 feet of water, let out lots of scope and tied the anchor line to my bow line. Just as I was attaching the ladder to the transom, I was knocked off balance and nearly thrown overboard. At first I thought something had hit the boat, but then I realized that something had hit the anchor line and jolted the boat.

While I was wondering what was going on, it happened again from a different direction. And then again, and again. Was it the manta? A couple of times on the fish finder I saw a huge blip, which must have been the manta swimming under the transducer. But why would it keep hitting my anchor line?

My little boat was getting thrashed around like a cork—kind of like a scene in the movie *Jaws.* Suddenly, the boat started moving in a straight line—at a good clip. I glanced at the depth finder and saw it going from 70 to 80, 90, 100, 110, 120 feet. The manta must have lifted the anchor off the bottom and was dragging me out to sea.

I couldn't imagine how this fish could be hooked up to my anchor. There is no tail to wrap up and the manta's shape doesn't lend itself to tangles. Finally, at 120 feet, everything stopped. The anchor line pointed straight down and seemed to be stuck on the bottom. I figured the manta must have freed itself but left me hooked up on the bottom, far from where I started, so I untied the anchor line from the bow line and started to heave on it, hoping to unhook the anchor. No luck. Next I tried letting out a bunch of slack and backing the boat up in several directions, but that didn't work. I was not looking forward to suiting up and diving down to 120 feet to pry the anchor free.

All at once, it started again. The manta took off with the boat, but now the anchor line wasn't attached to the bow—I was holding it. The line started slipping through my hands. I couldn't compete with the awesome power of this animal, and I couldn't tie the line off to the bow line because I was nowhere near it. My hands and arms shook with exhaustion, but I managed to attach the line to a cleat. That meant the manta was now pulling the boat through the water sideways at a respectable speed.

The situation was getting a bit scary. With all this thrashing around, I was afraid the rope would get tangled in the prop or ladder and do some serious damage. Then the momentum stopped again and the line went slack. But only for a second. I saw the big blip on the depth finder and knew the manta had turned around and was headed in the opposite direction.

I had seen some people in a zodiac and a Coast Guard cutter anchored in the bay earlier but had no luck trying to contact them on the CB. Just then the manta hit the end of the slack. The rope attached to the cleat was now going under the boat, and the impact was so hard I thought the rope might break or the cleat give way. Neither happened, but the boat leaned at such a steep angle as the manta dragged it through the water, I started to realize that this thing was strong enough to tip me over. This was not funny anymore.

I decided, "to hell with this. I can always get another anchor." I grabbed the emergency rope knife next to the wheel, cut the line and watched it disappear into the depths. For some time, I sat there breathing hard and wondering in disbelief how this could have happened. Perhaps the ray did a flip or sharp turn, hooked the anchor in the line, and looped itself in a knot. I didn't know. All I knew was that anchor was not about to fall off. At least the ray didn't take the anchor five minutes later when I would have been in the water, stranded offshore and watching my boat being towed out to sea.

With no anchor I couldn't dive, so I headed home, but not without stopping to catch two nice mahimahi near a floating log. I now have a new anchor and chain, and I hope the manta does not still have my old one. If you are swimming near Kealakekua Bay and see an anchor with about 150 feet of free yellow rope attached to it, you will know how it got there.

Contributed by Dale Sarver

Food for Thought

Back in September and October of 1999, while working on a report about the stomach contents of sharks, I went out boat fishing for nearshore sandbar, tiger and Galapagos sharks using bottom longline gear. Over Penguin Bank near Moloka'i, we caught a 13-foot tiger and in its stomach I found sea-turtle remains, turtle tags, octopus beaks and fish vertebrae. I also discovered a small, yellow plastic bird band, but not the type that would fit a boobie or albatross.

Turns out—thanks to investigative work by Beth Flint at the U.S. Fish and Wildlife office—that it belonged to a homing pigeon that raced between islands. The owners were surprised to find out that their prized racing pigeon had been eaten by a tiger shark. I also found several strands of human hair, which were later tested for DNA by the detective division of the Maui police department but didn't match up to any of their unsolved shark-attack cases.

Turtle shells and squid and turtle beaks are among the items found in a tiger shark's stomach.

On the same day we caught another tiger shark with yet another racing pigeon leg band in its stomach. Only this one was from a different race, I discovered, when I also found a numbered rubber band, used for time and start placement, that correlated with the plastic leg band.

While off Gardner Pinnacles on October 2, we caught a 14-foot tiger shark that had the following items in its stomach: sea-turtle remains, bird feathers, sea fan branches, a Bic lighter, 16 octopi beaks, a fishing leader, two pieces of rubber hose, three pieces of garbage bags, two different types of fishing nets (approximately 3 x 6 ft.) and a FIVE GALLON bucket. You could see the outline of the bucket in the shark's abdomen. Not quite the right food groups there but certainly an array of stuff. I guess it's true that tigers will eat just about anything.

Contributed by Andrew Vatter, National Marine Fisheries Service

Richard Pyle and his rebreather.

Bending the Rules

Note: The author dives with a rebreather—a diving apparatus that mixes oxygen, nitrogen and helium for deep-water, bubble-free dives.

On September 24, 1998, some friends and I embarked on a sail-boat cruise to tiny, remote Necker Island in the Northwestern Hawaiian Islands. We were to be gone for nine days—six days of travel there and back from Honolulu, and three days of diving. I had my rebreather with me, and the others planned to use regular scuba gear on mostly no- or mild-decompression dives.

When we arrived on Sunday, September 27, the water was crystal clear and the array of fish was utterly amazing, a spearfisher's dream. More gray snapper and large jacks than I have seen anywhere in human-inhabited Hawaiian waters, including Midway Atoll. Of course there were also lots and lots of sharks. Mostly whitetip reef, gray reef and Galapagos. I was amazed not only with the abundance of sharks but how close they came—perhaps because I was using the rebreather—and they were not at all aggressive.

Galapagos shark.

Necker, which is less than a mile long and a couple of hundred yards wide, is surrounded by an almost perfectly flat shelf ten miles in radius. Along the perimeter of this shelf is a ledge about 90-120 feet deep, and a stone's throw from the ledge is a precipitous drop-off to a thousand fathoms (6,000 feet) or more. Throughout my 90-minute afternoon dive on this ledge there were usually five-to-seven, four-to-six-foot Galapagos and a few other sharks in view at any given time.

Anyone who has spent a lot of time diving with sharks knows that they have a comfort zone of closeness to a diver, usually preferring to stay 8-12 feet away. Galapagos sharks have a closer comfort zone—more like 5-8 feet, but on this dive they were even closer and on many occasions I could have just reached up and petted them as they swam by. Although this was slightly disconcerting, they weren't showing any aggressive tendencies even when I collected fish specimens, so despite being alone (the scuba divers had already used up their precious bottom time), I wasn't terribly concerned. I ended the dive just before sunset, and as I came up the decompression (deco) line attached to the boat, the sharks followed me.

Gray reef shark.

All of a sudden, however, the largest shark charged at me, and I had to kick it off. Then another one charged, and another. For the next five minutes or so the seven or eight sharks surrounding me (within a ten-foot radius) started acting more and more agitated and taking turns at charges. Kicking them off wasn't working, so I clipped my catch bucket holding my specimens to the deco line and moved closer to the surface. This split the sharks between me and the bucket. They nuzzled it then took a turn at me. It was terribly unnerving, especially since the sun was setting and I was alone in the water. Finally, cutting short my decompression time by three or four minutes, I ended the dive. Back in the boat, I breathed pure oxygen for a few minutes just as a precaution.

The next day's dives were enjoyable but uneventful...that is, until the last dive of the day. At first it was magnificent, and so peaceful on the rebreather with no other divers around. After a quarter mile or so of finding all sorts of interesting ledges, overhangs, tunnels, etc., I ended up back at the boat anchor. This several-hundred-pound chunk of metal was connected to our 70-foot boat by a giant chain, but at the moment it was wedged deeply under a ledge at 90 feet and would be difficult to pull up, especially since the current had picked up considerably, as had the wind and the chop at the surface. Still, that was the boat captain's problem, I reasoned, as I swam up the anchor chain to the decompression line. Then suddenly.... BANG! It sounded like a gun shot. I looked up to see 2,000 pounds of chain sinking rapidly to the bottom and the boat drifting off. The chain had snapped near the bow of the boat.

There was less than an hour of daylight left. If we were to recover the anchor that day, we'd need to act quickly. Back on the boat (after cutting short my safety deco again) we devised a plan. I went back down and found the anchor. The boat crew dropped a two-inch-thick rope weighted with 40 pounds of lead, but because of the wind and current, the lead weight landed 80 feet from the anchor. For about ten minutes I dragged that 40-pound weight across a rocky bottom, fighting the pull of 300 feet of rope arching through 90 feet of water in a strong current. When I got it to within five feet, the boat started to drift off again. I signaled a free diver at the surface for more slack, but in the fading light he could barely see me and thought my signal meant hoist away. All that hard work for nothing as I watched the rope snake up towards the surface.

While I was waiting for the boat crew to realize the problem and get back into position, I decided to try and get the anchor clear of the ledge and down a slope, making recovery easier. With a great deal of effort, I freed the anchor after first gathering up about fifteen feet of heavy chain. Then, since the free diver could no longer see me in the dark, I had to break deco to surface and tell the boat crew where the anchor was. On the bottom again, I dragged the lead weight ten feet and shackled it to the anchor. Mission accomplished.

Now I had to finish my deco at about 30 feet, but I was worried about the boat crew finding me without a reference float (mine had floated away when its line snapped). Just then I saw a large gray reef shark approach. To my surprise, it came straight toward me and began classic threat-display posturing—pectoral fins pointing down, arched back, and swimming in a highly exaggerated figure eight—which these sharks do just before attacking. A friend of mine was confronted by a posturing gray reef shark once, and the shark ripped his arm apart, nearly killing him. With this in mind, I ignored my last few minutes of deco and got my ass back in the boat. Again, I grabbed some oxygen and inhaled it for nearly an hour. Lucky me, I thought. I cheated the bends once again.

We had a lot of fun talking about the exciting events of the day. I was a bit nervous about breaking deco two days in a row, especially since the heavy workload and long bottom times at 90-120 feet must be pushing my body tissues to the limit. You would think this would cause me to be extra super-duper careful for the remainder of the trip. You would think I would have thanked my lucky stars and chilled out a bit. You would think.

The next day was our last and I wanted to make it count. The boat was anchored at the mouth of a large underwater canyon with a pure-white sandy bottom—a very obvious landmark that would make it easy to find the anchor on my return. I hitched a ride several hundred yards up-current with two other divers on an underwater DPV, then left them to explore on my own. I stayed quite a long time collecting fish and checking out the reef, although I was working harder than usual to buck the current, which picked up a bit later in the day.

On the way back to the boat as I followed the ridge and underwater canyon, the topography looked pretty much like what I had remembered for the anchor spot, but there was no anchor. When I popped up to the surface to look for the boat, I was surprised to find it 250 feet behind me, up current. I had been following the wrong underwater canyon—there were two of them side by side.

I turned around to go back down and finish my deco on the way to the boat, but my heart nearly stopped as I found myself face to face (less than one foot away) with a large Galapagos shark. I kicked the shark and it veered away, but there were about seven more sharks between me and my bucket of fish and they were nastier than before. It was decision time in a miserable situation. If I waited the thirty minutes it would take for the boat to haul anchor and come and get me, in this strong current I would float out to sea in the dark. And if they couldn't find me, next stop, Marshall Islands.

Luckily I saw the stern line float only 30 or 40 feet away, so decided to go for it and finish deco under the boat. As I swam toward the stern line, the sharks followed. Between me and my bucket of fish 30 feet away were a bunch of dorsal fins and shark tails thrashing around. It was almost funny.

I decided to pretend the sharks weren't there since there wasn't a whole lot I could do about them. Fighting the current with all that gear and a 5-gallon bucket in tow was an extremely hard 5-minute swim, but I finally got there and took a moment to relax and assess how I felt. My stomach felt a bit ill (likely due to swallowing sea water, I reasoned) and I was a bit short of breath, but otherwise ok. I mustered the courage to look back at the sharks, which was a mistake because they were still agitated and one was heading towards me. Most of them, however, were bumping the bucket. At least they weren't bumping me.

I quickly pulled myself along the stern line back to the boat while the crew hauled in the fish bucket, but now what to do about decompression. I needed another 30 minutes at 30 feet down. But when I got on the boat to assess the shark versus deco situation, my abdomen started painfully cramping up and I was getting shorter and shorter of breath. Grabbing an oxygen cylinder under my arm, I rolled over the side of the boat into the ocean, breathing hard and coughing violently (classic bends symptoms). Twenty minutes later, I was feeling better, but the sharks were still hanging around and it was almost dark, so I got back in the boat.

That's when it really hit. My eyes weren't focusing and my hands became uncoordinated. In less than sixty seconds, the symptoms increased dramatically. Now I couldn't walk. My legs and arms were useless. I gasped for help. "Put my fins on." Someone did. "Put a mask on." Someone did, and I managed to roll myself over the side again—just a lump of flotsam bobbing on the surface, struggling to keep my head above water and fearing I would drown. Scott jumped in and held me at the surface while others got the oxygen ready. By then, near paralysis and not able to submerge, I agreed to be hauled back into the boat—no easy task in choppy waves with the boat pitching heavily.

The next three and a half days were a nightmare. As we motored to distant Honolulu, site of the nearest decompression chamber, I went through hell. In a bunk below deck I fought to insert an intravenous needle in my right arm and to keep it there—and me in the bunk— while the boat pitched and rolled 45 degrees in 12-15 foot seas. The smell of the head and the engine's diesel fumes made me vomit, and pulmonary oxygen toxicity (irritation in the lungs, shortness of breath, coughing and nausea) kicked in from all the canned, open-circuit, doctor-ordered oxygen I was inhaling. After eight hours of oxygen, I thought I was going to die as I worried about pulmonary edema—when the lungs get so irritated that the alveoli start to fill with fluid. That's when I decided to stop the oxygen and take my chances. It worked. Gradually, I improved and by the time we reached O'ahu I was weak but much better and could skip the decompression chamber. As I look back on this experience, I realize I made dozens of little mistakes—not having a compass with me on a distance-swimming dive, or a small, inflatable chase boat ready to go, or perhaps a shark protection device. But I also made one BIG mistake: I didn't take a 120-foot dive seriously because I was used to dives at 400 feet with the rebreather. Let's hope I've learned my lesson.

Contributed by Richard Pyle

The Battle for the Bull

While operating a fishing charter on the 38-foot Pacific Safari on October 9, 1992, Captain Marc Minkler, crew member Moki Bergau, and passenger Dr. Phillip Adams from Houston, Texas, saw an amazing sight. Several 14-foot and larger tiger sharks surrounded a 2,000-pound bull swimming about 2-1/2 miles offshore, 7 miles south of Hāna, Maui, and ripped it apart in the space of about ten minutes, while the fishermen tried to get a rope around its neck and drag it to safety. It seems that the sharks won the battle. The largest shark swallowed the bull's entire head in one gulp, and then when the bull had been picked apart by the others, came back for the remaining 500-pound piece, swimming under the glass-bottom boat with its prize.

The bull's owner, Henry Rost of Hāna, figured that it had slipped down the pali, and with no fresh water available and not able to climb back up, must have headed out to sea as a last resort.

Contributed by Hawaii Fishing News

Friendly Sharks

It was March 19, 2001, and we were heading out on a charter south of Kona with ten clients (a full boatload). We often venture a few miles off shore in hopes of spotting a big critter or two—usually pilot whales—and as usual, we were in luck. Only half an hour into our trip, we saw a group of twenty or so pilot whales just lazing on the surface. After watching them for awhile to see what they would do, and after noting that they were spy hopping to check us out, we decided to try and swim with them on snorkel. The pilot whales, however, wanted nothing to do with us, and when we got into the water and too close for comfort, they moved away to a safe distance.

It wasn't long, though, until Mark (one of our crew members) called out my favorite five-letter word—shark! Sure enough, a beautiful, female, six-foot oceanic whitetip was approaching us at the surface in the company of two blue-and-black-striped pilot-fish. Bold behavior is a trademark of this shark species and one of the reasons I love swimming with them. She swam right up to us, then did a lazy turn to check out the boat.

I wasn't surprised to see this magnificent animal because we very often see oceanic whitetips following the pilot whales. But I WAS surprised when a client yelled my name and I swung around to find myself face to fin with another oceanic coming from behind

Kendra poses as a shark.

Kendra and Dive Makai Charters mascot Little Bits, who loves to bark at sharks.

and trying to surprise me. The minute I turned, the shark (another female) did a quick 180. Another shark approached Mark, but it wasn't an oceanic. We think it was a silky. It made one pass and then we never saw it again.

Now we had five oceanics in view—all female as far as I could tell and all about six feet long. Two never approached us closely—they looked very robust and pregnant. The first shark was more than obliging though, and the three of us with cameras were eagerly snapping away. She took a special interest in one client, Mike, who carried a big camera with two strobes. In my experience with these sharks, they seem to be drawn to big cameras—possibly because of the electric field produced by batteries, circuitry and metal in water. She approached him slowly but just kept coming at him. If he didn't bump her in the nose with his camera, she bumped him. And she kept doing this repeatedly, like she was testing us. Perhaps she wanted to see if we were a potential meal (by not pushing her back, we might be considered prey?). She chased me out of the water twice (she was just too close for comfort without a big camera to hide behind) and chased the others out, too. But we kept getting back in, and she waited for us—circling the boat if we were all out of the water. Underwater we still had to watch out for other sharks in the area. They kept making close passes at us when our backs were turned.

From the boat I could still see the pilot whales in the distance, and among all the black whale fins, there was a bright white fin—an oceanic whitetip shark hanging out amidst the whales. I threw a cookie in the water to see what our sharks would do, but they just sniffed it with little interest. The pilot fish, however, devoured the snack eagerly. When we finally started the engines, our first curious shark was still circling the boat, but it was time to move on and see if we could find a dive site.

Twenty minutes later we slipped in with another pod of pilot whales (two big bulls, females and even a few baby calves) basking on the surface, and they were much less skittish, letting us swim behind them for about ten minutes. Three oceanic whitetip sharks accompanied this pod of whales, so the shark count for the day was nine and we hadn't even done a dive yet. Everybody was thrilled to be able to swim with such curious, magnificent creatures who accepted our presence (probably out of curiosity) and interacted with us on their own accord. They are truly masters of their environment and should be respected and appreciated for what they are—apex predators necessary to ensure the health and vitality of the ocean.

Contributed by Kendra Choquette of Dive Makai Charters

CHAPTER 12

PROTECTING SHARKS AND RAYS

Courtesy of NMFS/PIAO.

A modern longliner nooses a shark around its gills.

It's hard to imagine sharks and rays needing protection, but that's no longer such a farfetched idea. In the not-too-distant past, when the phrase, "the only good shark is a dead shark," was in vogue, sharks were branded a nuisance and killed without a second thought. Such was the case in the early 1900s when Young Brothers routinely hung sharks up by their tails on the dock in Honolulu. Even today, an estimated twelve million sharks a year are killed worldwide....for their fins, for food, or just because they're sharks.

Eating sharks? The idea seems unappealing to most of us, but for people in some parts of the world, sharks make up at least a portion of their diet. To meet the demand, fisheries specializing in sharks spring up in these areas, only to find themselves out of business a few years later when shark populations dwindle under the fishing pressure. In the 1970s, researcher M.J. Holden raised doubts about the possibility of sustaining high-level shark fisheries after noticing the boom and bust cycles of tope (*Galeorhinus galeus*), basking (*Cetorhinus maximus*), piked dogfish (*Squalus acanthias*), and porbeagle (*Lamna nasus*) shark fisheries around the world.

A 16-foot shark hangs in a shed on Honolulu's wharf in 1907.

No shark fisheries exist in Hawai'i, but at one time, shark meat was sold in the Islands under the name grayfish or added to fishcake—a 21,000-pound-a-year industry between 1944 and 1953. When a Hawai'i State Department of Health ruling called for accurate ingredient labeling, many unhappy consumers learned that they had been eating shark, and fishcake sales plummeted to 200 pounds in 1954 and 12 pounds in 1955. Sales of fishcake also sank "whenever there was news that a human being had been bitten or eaten by a shark," noted George Akau, chief of the health department's food and drug branch (as reported in the Honolulu Advertiser, July 14, 1970). With drooping sales, the practice of using shark meat in fishcake floundered, and as a result, the coastal population of sharks around the Hawaiian Islands is higher than in many areas of the world—a fact that undoubtedly helps maintain the diversity and stability of Hawai'i's marine environment.

Right: A net takes its toll on this scalloped hammerhead.

Dried shark fins.

Even in a stable environment, Hawai'i's sharks face hazards. Until recently, tuna fishery operations caught sharks mainly as bycatch, but with the rising demand for shark-fin soup, fishing boat captains targeted large numbers of sharks for their fins. In 1998 Hawai'i's offshore longline fisheries brought in more than a million dollars worth of fins. With little or no regulation, such lucrative rewards could drastically reduce the pelagic shark population in the North Pacific. To offset that possibility, Hawai'i passed legislation in the year 2000 making it mandatory for fishermen to bring the whole shark carcass into port before it can be finned. No longer can a shark's fins be cut off and the carcass dumped overboard. With no room to store bulky, unsalable blue shark meat (blue sharks make up the majority of sharks finned), fishing boats will likely use their limited freezer space for more valuable stores of tuna and other food fish, and the legislation will have served its purpose—reducing the killing of sharks just for their fins.

Faced with increasing evidence that shark populations worldwide face declining numbers, several countries have instituted regulations and protected-species management plans. In April 1991 the South African Minister of Environment Affairs took the unprecedented step of protecting the great white shark in the economic zone of South Africa. The new legislation made it illegal to catch or kill any great white shark without a permit, or to sell or offer for sale any great white shark product. Great whites, an object of hysteria following the 1975 movie, *Jaws*, are also protected off the U.S. coast of California, and by the Australian states of New

NOTICE
SHARK FINNING LAW
NOW IN EFFECT

It is now unlawful to knowingly harvest shark fins from State waters, or land shark fins in the State regardless of the waters in which the sharks were caught, unless the fins were taken from a shark that was landed whole in the State.

Penalties include:
• seizure and forfeiture of shark fins, commercial marine license, fishing vessel, fishing equipment, as well as
• administrative fines of not less than $5,000, not more than $15,000, plus administrative and attorney's fees and costs.

The new law applies to:
• vessels with federal documentation listing as a homeport a location within the State,
• undocumented vessels registered and numbered by the State, and
• vessels holding a fishing license or permit issued by the State allowing them to participate in a fishery, or having owners or captains holding a fishing license or permit issued by the State allowing them to participate in a fishery.

Department of Land and Natural Resources
Division of Aquatic Resources

Hawai'i's legislature passed a shark-finning law in 2000.

Great white sharks are protected in some areas of the world.

Two Australian states protect sand tiger sharks.

South Wales and Victoria. Also in Australia, New South Wales and Queensland protect sand tiger sharks (*Carcharias taurus*); and several countries mandate species bag limits as well as seasonal and area closures that protect sharks either directly or indirectly.

The 'K' Strategy

One reason that sharks need protection is because they reproduce by what is known as the 'K' strategy of population growth. Biologists recognize two types of reproductive strategies: The 'r' strategy applies to many bony fish, who grow quickly to maturity, reproduce often and produce hundreds, thousands or even millions of eggs that are discharged into the water then left alone to develop and grow into adults. Most sharks and rays follow the opposite, or 'K,' strategy. Because they grow slowly, produce relatively few well-developed young, and take many years to reach reproductive age, these sharks and rays cannot withstand heavy fishing pressure. Human beings reach reproductive age after completing only 18% of a normal life span. The bigeye thresher shark, on the other hand, must live out 60% of her life span, surviving natural predation and dangers such as fishing hooks and nets, before she can bear young (sexual maturity at 12 years, with a life span of 20 years).

A crocodile shark gives birth to only four pups at a time, and not all of them will survive.

Having reigned for 400-million years as the ocean's top predator, sharks are now vulnerable in the wake of improved fishing methods that remove large numbers of them from the sea at an ever-increasing rate. The tope shark, for example, might live to a ripe old age of 50 but because of its K-selected reproduction traits,

The shortspine spurdog shark population at Hawai'i's Hancock Seamount decreased by 50% over a four-year fishing period.

can sustain only a 2-3% per year decline in numbers for its population to remain stable. In Hawai'i, a survey conducted by the National Marine Fisheries Service discovered that between 1985 and 1988, the shortspine spurdog shark population over the Hancock Seamount had decreased by fifty percent, according to fisheries' catch rates.

Removing sharks leaves the ocean unbalanced, and that results in some inevitable complications. When a lobster fishery in Tasmania expanded to include gummy sharks (*Mustelus antarcticus*), a natural predator of the octopus, the octopus population (which feeds on lobsters) increased and the number of lobsters dropped rapidly. This example vividly shows how interrelated life in the sea can be, and how weakening one strand of such a complex web causes other strands to collapse like a row of dominoes.

Shark Control

Shark-control programs have resulted in some interesting consequences for shark conservation efforts in Hawai'i. From the late 1950s through the 1970s, Hawai'i's government-funded shark-control efforts removed 2,849 sharks (excluding pups) from the ocean. These programs allowed researchers to gather valuable information about shark species and increase their understanding of the ocean environment—an understanding that will no doubt aid shark and ocean preservation efforts in the future.

In the early 1990s, two fatal (suspected tiger) shark attacks and several other shark-related incidents brought the shark-control issue into the limelight once again. In response, the newly created Hawai'i Shark Task Force adopted a limited shark-control program and conducted research that would help officials better understand the tiger shark's movement patterns. "It was clear at task-force meetings that we knew very little about the tiger shark," explains task-force member Gerald Crow, "and that just removing sharks from the ocean wasn't going to solve the problem. At that time, we didn't know how and when they reproduced or the extent of their home ranges. We didn't even know for sure whether or not tiger sharks were territorial, as had been previously assumed."

To solve the home-range and territorial questions, task-force members asked Kim Holland of the Hawai'i Institute of Marine Biology to apply his tuna-tracking methods and technology to tiger sharks. Data from sonic transmitters affixed to the sharks' dorsal fins or inserted in body cavities, and records from sea-floor monitors that listened for a shark's return to a selected site revealed that tiger sharks roam between islands—much farther than previously thought. The sharks occasionally swam past the

An ultrasonic transmitter implanted in a shark's body cavity sends signals to this bottom monitor, which stores the information until it can be downloaded to a computer.

monitors but were often absent for long periods of time. In addition, Holland and his O'ahu-based crew tracked several sharks to Penguin Bank near Moloka'i and found that one shark had traveled to Kona. This information implied that tiger sharks patrol large home ranges and that removing them from a limited area would probably not be effective in protecting coastal areas around Hawai'i.

Swimming With Sharks and Rays

Ecotourism plays a part in helping us understand, appreciate and protect sharks and rays. In particular, diving and snorkeling with sharks, a pastime that would have seemed foolhardy only twenty years ago, is now a fast-growing recreational activity. Publications such as Time Life Books' *Sharks and Rays* list dive shop and tour operators around the world who take visitors into the ocean to observe great white sharks from a cage, swim with feeding reef sharks, and pet and feed stingrays, among other close encounters. In Hawai'i, some dive operators on the Big Island offer dives with gray reef and oceanic whitetip sharks, as well as manta ray snorkeling and dive tours. Also on the Big Island at the Four Seasons Resort at Hualalai, guests can swim and snorkel with spotted eagle rays in the ray lagoon or hand-feed the gentle animals at specific feeding times.

"Where did that shark go?" asks a snorkeler, as a curious oceanic whitetip wonders what strange creature has invaded its home.

A great white shark surveys a diver in a cage.

Jeff Rotman/Innerspace Visions

Free divers hitch a ride with a whale shark in Moanalua Bay circa 1975.

Lyman Higa

Visitors watch as children and adults take turns feeding spotted eagle rays at the Four Seasons Hualalai ray lagoon.

Gerald Crow

Recreational cage-diving and shark-feeding activities are exciting but also controversial because we don't know how artificial feeding at dive sites might alter the behavior of sharks. Will they become less wary of people? Or more aggressive, viewing humans as a source of food? Until recently, visitors delighted in feeding peas to the fish in O'ahu's Hanauma Bay. Over time though, observers noticed that larger, more aggressive fish took the place of smaller butterflyfish, wrasses and tangs, changing the bay's ecosystem. When these upstart arrivals demanded food by biting swimmers' legs and hands, officials eliminated the fish-feeding practice, thus encouraging the aggressive fish to look for food elsewhere. It might take some time, but the restoration process has begun, and Hanauma Bay will eventually attract its original diversity of marine life.

A diver watches a Galapagos shark swim by in Moanalua Bay (1978).

Lyman Higa

Protection from Sharks

With an increase in ocean recreation worldwide, the possibility of dangerous encounters with sharks also increases. To make the ocean a safer place for swimmers, snorkelers, divers and others, and to avoid slaughtering sharks in retribution for an attack, several shark-protective devices are on the market or in various stages of testing.

One such device, the Johnson shark bag—named for its inventor, C. Scott Johnson, and created while he was working for the U.S. Navy—consists of a large bag with a floatable top. Designed for sea disasters involving U.S. military personnel, the shapeless bag hides its occupant from patrolling sharks until help arrives. Jacques Cousteau tested the bag in the Indian Ocean and found that sharks circled close enough to deliberately bump the bag several times. Fearing for the safety of the diver in the bag, and unsure of what the sharks would do next, Cousteau aborted the test and pulled the diver out of harm's way.

A chain-mail suit developed by Ron and Valerie Taylor and Jeremiah Sullivan contains 400,000 interlocking stainless-steel rings and has been effective as a deterrent to serious bites. However, glove connection problems can leave hands and wrists vulnerable, and the suit cannot prevent crushing damage from the force of a severe bite.

The compact, lightweight Shark POD (Protective Ocean Device) works by disrupting a shark's electric-field detection system (see **Chapter 3: Senses**). Tests of the Shark POD show promise and studies are ongoing, however a shark in an aggressive feeding mode rushing toward its prey might not be able to slow its forward trajectory in time to respond to the electric deterrent.

Common sense can go a long way towards keeping us safe from shark attacks, as the sidebar on the next page shows (safety tips contributed by Hawaiian historian Herb Kane and the Department of Land and Natural Resources' Division of Aquatic Resources).

Reduce the Risk of Shark Attacks:

Ten Safety Tips

1 Never go swimming, surfing or diving alone.

2 Dawn, dusk and night are feeding times for many sharks; avoid the water during these times.

3 If you are bleeding or have open wounds, stay out of the water. Sharks can smell even small amounts of blood and body fluids.

4 Avoid places where you'll most likely find sharks: harbor entrances, near stream mouths (especially after heavy rains) and other murky water; and channels or steep drop-offs.

5 Don't wear bright-colored clothes or shiny jewelry into the ocean; sharks can see these very well.

6 Splashing attracts sharks; so do pets in the water.

7 Don't provoke or harass even a small shark, and leave the water quickly if warned that sharks are around, even if you don't see them.

8 Leave the water if fish or turtles behave erratically; they can tell if a shark is nearby.

9 Don't swim near anyone fishing; hooked and speared fish or other dead animals can attract sharks.

10 Pay attention to lifeguards; they're familiar with the territory.

Ambush predators, sharks prefer to attack their victims from behind, as the authors found out firsthand while snorkeling outside Midway Atoll's lagoon in the Northwestern Hawaiian Islands. At one point, three Galapagos sharks approached a member of our group as she attempted to photograph a colorful fish. At first they idled a few feet away, watching her, but when one started to inch closer, instinct urged her to turn around and face her stalkers. With the element of surprise gone and their potential prey's eyes looking at them, the sharks turned tail and swam away. This face-to-face method of preventing an ambush also worked successfully to avert Bengal tiger attacks in India. On treks through the jungle, the last person in line often disappeared until trail walkers attached face masks to the backs of their heads, visually eliminating the predator's ability to ambush without warning. The ruse worked, drastically cutting down on the number of tiger attacks.

Divers watch a whitetip reef shark under the cargo pier at Midway Atoll.

Although sharks don't always attack in clear water where they can potentially see their victim's eyes, could such a mask experiment prove effective with sharks? At the very least, it might be worth a try. Researcher Howard Hall, working in Australia, noticed that great white sharks backed off when he left the safety of the cage and approached them. However, they persistently tried to maneuver behind his back.

Looking Towards the Future

Tiger sharks play an important role in the ocean environment.

In the debate between shark fishing and conservation, it's clear we still have a lot to learn. As the gummy shark, octopus and lobster example shows, including sharks in fisheries can potentially harm the ecosystem unless we develop a clearer view of each species' reproductive strategy and the impact of its removal on other aspects of ocean life. We must take a closer look at how widely sharks and rays are distributed, where they live, what factors influence their choice of habitat and how fishing will affect that habitat before we can make informed choices affecting either side of the conservation issue.

Fortunately, attitudes about sharks are changing. Even the once-vilified tiger shark now enjoys an improved image thanks to research into its life cycle, habitat and behavior. Sharks and rays have a vital role to play in the complex marine environment, and learning more about them will allow us to become effective stewards of the oceans. Shark protection, unthinkable twenty years ago, is a reality today because research has provided us with valuable insights into the lives of these fascinating animals. Ultimately, what we understand, we care about, and what we care about, we protect.

Getting along with sharks can seem difficult at times, but the more we understand these unique animals, the more we will appreciate them.

Glossary

aileron Movable part on the back edge of an airplane wing; raised or lowered, especially noticeable on landing, it gives the pilot lateral control of the plane.

ampullae of Lorenzini Electric-sense receptors; they measure minute changes to the electric field around animals.

anal fin Single fin behind the cloaca; can be absent or present, depending on the species.

anthranillic acid Crystalline acid used as an intermediate step in the manufacture of dyes, pharmaceuticals, and perfumes. Can also be used as a marker to confirm the presence of squalene.

aplacental Lit. without a placenta. In a female shark or ray's uterus, each embryo relies primarily on the substantial yolk in its initial egg (one egg only), or many eggs (oophagous) for development.

appendiculae Finger-like projections on the umbilical cord in those sharks that use a placenta (i.e. hammerhead in Hawai'i).

archipelago A group of islands.

atoll Ring-shaped chain of coral reefs from which a few low islands project above the sea's surface.

bank Raised underwater geologic surface. Penguin Bank west of Moloka'i is a separate, submersed volcano covered with a carbonate deposit.

basal plate An anchoring part that holds the scale in place in the dermis.

basalt Igneous rock, dark gray-to-black and dense-to-fine-grained, made of basic plagioclase, augite, and usually magnetite; often of volcanic origin.

bathypelagic The lower part of the ocean; a zone just above the sea floor at depths of 3,280 to 13,120 feet.

bioluminescence Glowing light, sometimes green. Emitted by light-producing organs on the bodies of some animals (e.g. cookiecutter sharks, flashlight fish, fireflies). Practically heatless light is produced by bacteria, or when pigments are oxidized in the presence of certain enzymes.

Carcharhinid Scientific classification: group of fifty sharks from the family Carcharhinidae.

carchatoxin A and B A not-fully-understood compound that might be a form of ciguatoxin (ciguatera). It was found in the muscle and liver of a bull shark and caused 50 deaths.

centra Circular portions of a backbone or spine (singular: centrum).

cephalic horns Broad flaps on either side of the mouth of filter-feeding manta and devil rays; used to help channel zooplankton into the mouth.

cephalofoil A broad head that produces lift and stability while swimming. Usually applied to hammerhead sharks.

cephalopod Lit. head-footed. A group of animals with legs attached to the head; includes cuttlefish, squid, and octopus.

chondrocranium Skull made of cartilage, found in sharks, skates, rays, and chimerids.

ciguatera Toxic poison produced by dinoflagellates in fish. Eating ciguatera-contaminated fish results in symptoms of poisoning in humans.

claspers Modified, cigar-shaped portions of the pelvic fins in male sharks and rays; used for transporting sperm to the female.

clasper flexion Actively pumping a clasper back and forth prior to mating as a way of filling the siphon sac with seawater.

clasper groove A slit in the inner edge of the clasper. This groove allows seawater from the siphon sac in male sharks (or clasper gland secretions in male rays) to mix with sperm from the urogential papillae and pass into the female.

cloaca Common opening for digestive, urinary, and reproductive tracts in many fish.

conicospiral A type of valvular intestine in which the valves wind around a central column and are attached to the intestine walls.

countershading Coloration pattern in which the upper surface is darkly pigmented and the sides and ventral surface are silvery or only lightly pigmented.

crustacean Major group of animals with shells, including crabs, shrimp, and lobsters.

cusplet Small pointed projection at the base and on either side of a tooth.

dental lamina Area of tooth formation and growth.

dermal denticles Small, tooth-like structures on the skin. Scales on the skin of sharks and other cartilaginous fish.

dorsal Upper part or surface, back, or top of an animal.

dorsal fin One or two unpaired fins along the back of fish and marine mammals.

electroreception Ability to detect electric fields produced by living organisms.

embryonic diapause Dormant period between the time an egg is fertilized and when the embryo is formed and begins to grow.

epipelagic Upper part of the ocean; a zone from the surface to about 760 feet deep.

euphausiid shrimp Small, pelagic, shrimp-like crustaceans.

fin spines Single, stout, pointed spine at the front of the dorsal fins of some sharks.

gastric eversion Expelling the stomach outside the body and pulling it back inside. A natural process, possibly used for cleaning the stomach of unwanted objects. Observed, mainly by fishermen, in sharks that have long pyloric stomachs, usually when the shark has been fighting on the line.

gill arches Cartilaginous arches supporting the gills.

gill filaments Flat blade-like extensions of red gill tissue where oxygen and carbon dioxide exchange takes place; filaments project from the gill arch.

gill rakers Finger-like projections on the gill arch that strain and capture food for filter-feeding sharks and rays; located on the opposite side from the red gill filaments.

gill slits A series of long narrow openings leading to the gills.

geomagnetic Magnetic field generated by the earth.

heterocercal Caudal (tail) fin shape in which the upper lobe is larger than the lower. This type of tail provides forward movement and slightly upward thrust.

hydrodynamic lift Lift generated by sharks and rays while swimming through water.

intestinal eversion A natural process whereby the intestine is forcibly expelled outside the body through the cloaca, flushed, and pulled back inside. Observed only in species with a scroll-valve intestine.

keel A firm, fleshy ridge; often related to a skin fold on the caudal peduncle (base of the tail) of some sharks and bony fish.

lagena One of the semicircular fluid-filled canals monitoring balance in the inner ear.

lamnid Scientific classification: a group of sharks from the family Lamnidae; includes the great white, longfin and shortfin makos, porbeagle, and salmon sharks.

lateral line A canal filled with hairs that detect nearby water movements and send signals to the brain. Pores on the skin allow water to pass into the canal.

luminescent See bioluminescence above.

macula neglecta Hearing center containing a large number of hair cells that sense and locate a sound source; located on the sacculus.

mechano-sensory Sensory systems that are physically triggered by water movement (including sound traveling through water) or contact with a physical object.

melanophores Cells on the body that contain melanin—a dark brown or black pigment. In sharks, these cells can expand and contract to darken or lighten the body.

mesopelagic Middle part of the ocean; a zone between 760 and 3,280 feet deep.

Midway Atoll For visitor information, go to www.midwayisland.com, or call toll free 1-888-643-9291.

NMFS observers Employees of the National Marine Fisheries Service who accompany fishing boats to record the types and numbers of fish, turtles, birds and marine mammals caught.

neuromasts Mechanical receptors of the lateral line or pit organs.

nictitating membrane A transparent, movable membrane or inner eyelid that protects the eye and keeps it clean.

nutritive eggs Infertile eggs that serve as additional food during embryo development.

oophagous A method of embryonic nutrition in which an embryo feeds on unfertilized eggs released by the mother into the uterus.

operculum Bony plate that covers and protects the gills in bony fishes. It opens to let water exit after passing over the gills.

ostium Funnel-shaped opening that allows eggs into the reproductive tract of female sharks.

oviduct Tube that connects the ostium to the oviducal gland, allowing eggs to pass through, in female sharks.

oviducal gland Where eggs are fertilized and wrapped or encapsulated. Sperm can be stored in this gland for just a few days or up to a year.

oviparous Producing eggs that hatch after being ejected from the body of the parent female.

pelagic Free swimming in a sea, ocean or other body of open water, not in association with the sea floor.

pectoral fins Paired fins just behind or below the gill openings; united to form a disc in most rays.

pelvic fins Paired fins (rarely joined) on the ventral surface between the head and vent or cloaca; sometimes called ventral fins.

pheromones Chemical substances used for communication between organisms of the same species.

pineal organ Light-reception area on top of the brain; may be used for light detection during seasonal and vertical migrations, and for adaptation of body coloration in response to light (see melanophores).

pit organs Contain neuromasts that help detect water movement over the skin. Located on the surface of the skin either in grooves (rays) or between modified scales (sharks).

placenta Tube- or stalk-like attachment from the embryo to the uterine lining; a conduit for food and wastes.

placoid scales Plate-like; applied to modified scales in sharks, rays, skates, and some extinct fish

predator An animal that feeds on other animals.

prey An animal taken by a predator as food.

pup A young shark or ray.

rete mirable Lit. wonderful net. An extensive network of minute blood vessels that serves a variety of functions in vertebrates, including as a heat exchanger.

ring valve A type of valvular intestine in which the valves are arranged like flat washers and are connected to the intestine wall.

sacculus The largest of three semicircular canals in the inner ear. Sharks and rays with a small sacculus tend to have poor sound-detection abilities.

sandcay Low island or reef of sand or coral.

scroll valve A type of valvular intestine in which the valves are not connected to the center and look like rolled up paper.

septum An extension of the gill arch, the septum separates each gill filament. In sharks and rays the gill septum supports the gill slits.

serotonin Chemical that inhibits gastric secretions and stimulates smooth muscle. A vasoconstrictor.

siphon sacs Muscular sacs located on the inner abdomen wall of male sharks. Siphon sacs fill up with seawater prior to mating and expel that water during mating, flushing the semen into the female.

spiracle Respiratory opening behind the eye, allowing water to flow over the gills; may be present or absent.

squalene A lipid that accumulates in large fat vacuoles in shark liver cells and can provide buoyancy in water. It might have medical uses and is also found in olive oil.

steroidal antibiotic A steroid with the ability to kill bacteria.

submersibles Vessels that operate underwater.

swim bladder A gas-filled organ that enables bony fish to adjust their buoyancy in the water.

tapetum lucidum Reflecting plates that act like mirrors behind the retina to reflect light back through the retina, helping to increase visual sensitivity.

tectonic A theory that the earth's crust consists of plates that are created at one end of their movement pattern and destroyed at the other end. The movement of the Pacific Plate affects the development and movement of the Hawaiian Islands.

thermocline An unstable, constantly shifting subsurface water mass characterized by rapid temperature change from its upper to lower surfaces.

trophonemata Longish finger-like projections extending from the uterine lining; they secrete a milk-like fluid.

urogenital opening A general opening in the cloaca where urine and sexual products are expelled from the body.

utriculus One of three semicircular canals in the inner ear; connected with balance coordination.

ventral Pertaining to the lower part or underneath of an animal.

vertical migration Behavior in which an animal swims toward the ocean's surface (often at sunset) and later reverses direction (often at sunrise). Normally associated with feeding.

visual streak A horizontal band in the retina of some sharks. It contains a higher cone and ganglion-cell density.

viviparous Producing live young from within the body of the parent female.

Glossary: Hawaiian

'ahi Hawaiian tuna, especially the yellow-fin tuna (*Thunnus albacares*).

akua God, goddess, spirit, ghost, devil, image, idol, corpse, supernatural.

akua manō God in the form of a shark.

ama Outrigger float, made of wiliwili wood (light wood also used for surfboards and net floats) and shaped in an arch so that the front and back ends were high and the body straight. The outrigger booms held it to the canoe. Also the port hull of a double canoe, so-called because it replaces the float.

'aumākua Family or personal gods; deified ancestors who might assume the shape of sharks, owls or other physical objects. 'Aumākua warned and reprimanded mortals in dreams and visions.

'awa Kava (*Piper methysticum*), a shrub 1.2 to 3.5 m tall with green jointed stems and heart-shaped leaves, native to Pacific islands. The root is the source of a narcotic drink of the same name used in ceremonies, prepared formerly by chewing, later by pounding. The chewed and pounded particles were mixed with water and strained. When drunk to excess it caused drowsiness and occasionally scaliness of the skin and bloodshot eyes. Kava was also used medicinally.

heiau Ancient Hawaiian place of worship. Some were elaborately constructed stone platforms, others simple earth terraces. They had various uses: treating the sick, making offerings to insure bountiful crops or good fishing, performing services to bring success in war, and for human sacrifice. Many are preserved today.

hīhīmanu Sting rays (*Dasyatidae*) and eagle rays (*Actobatus narinari*). Also called lupe.

imu Underground oven.

kahu Honored attendant, guardian, nurse, keeper, administrator, warden, caretaker, master. According to J.S. Emerson 92:2, kahu "implies the most intimate and confidential relations between the god and its guardian or keeper, while the word kahuna suggests more of the professional relation of the priest to the community."

kahu manō Shark caretaker.

kahuna Priest, sorcerer, magician, wizard, minister, expert in any profession (e.g. doctor, surgeon, dentist, agricultural expert, carving expert or sculptor, canoe builder).

kākū'ai To sacrifice food (fish, bananas, kava) to the gods; to feed the spirits of the dead; to deify a dead relative by food offerings and prayer; to dedicate the dead to become family protectors; to transfigure.

kapu Taboo, prohibited, sacredness, forbidden, no trespassing, keep out.

kīhei Shawl, cape, afghan, cloak, rectangular tapa garment worn over one shoulder and tied in a knot.

kukui Candlenut tree (*Aleurites moluccana*), a large tree bearing nuts containing white, oily kernels which were used for lights; hence the tree is a symbol of enlightenment. The nuts are still cooked for a relish. The soft wood was used for canoes, and gum from the bark for painting tapa; black dye was obtained from nut coats and from roots. Nuts were chewed and spat into the sea by fishermen to briefly create a clear surface for viewing, especially parrotfish. Polished nuts are strung in leis; the silvery leaves and small white flowers are strung in leis as representative of Moloka'i, as designated in 1923 by the Territorial legislature. The kukui was named the official emblem for the State of Hawai'i in 1959 because of its many uses and its symbolic value. Lamp, light, torch.

kūmanō To catch sharks with bait and noose (Malo 210, 213); also to set in order, as in laying stones; water dam, reservoir.

kupua Demigod or culture hero, especially a supernatural being possessing several forms (shark man).

kupuna Grandparent, ancestor, relative or close friend of the grandparent's generation. An adopted grandparent.

lupe Stingray or eagle ray; bird kite, kite with wings on the side (lupe manu).

malihini Stranger, foreigner, newcomer, tourist, guest, company, one unfamiliar with a place or custom, of foreign origin.

manō Shark. There were many types of sharks: *manō i'a* (ordinary shark), *manō hae* (fierce shark or fighter), *manō kanaka* (shark thought to be born of a human mother and sired by a shark god, or by a deified person whose spirit possesses a shark or turns into a shark), *manō ihu wa'a* (shark traditionally said to rest its head on the outrigger of a canoe, beloved by fishermen and fed).

manō hi'ukā Thresher shark (*Alopias pelagicus*); lit: tail-hitting shark

manō kanaka Shark man. Thought to be born of a human mother and sired by a shark god or by a deified person whose spirit possesses a shark or who turns into a shark.

manō kihikihi Hammerhead (*Sphryna lewini*); lit: angular shark.

manō lālākea Whitetip reef shark. Lit: white-fin shark.

manō lau kāhi'u Possibly thresher; lit: shark that frequently strikes tail.

moelua Striped, of two colors of about same width and lying parallel. A pattern of tapa.

mo'o Lizard, reptile of any kind, dragon, serpent, water spirit, enchanter.

niuhi Man-eating shark. Its flesh was taboo to women. Catching niuhi was the game of chiefs; it was a dangerous sport and special techniques were used.

'opihi Limpets, edible (often raw), pried off rocks.

pakaiea Sea lettuce. A variety of sugar cane; named for the seaweed; a variety of taro; name of a wind at Wai'anae.

tapa cloth Also called kapa; made from *wauke* or *mamaki* bark; formerly clothes of any kind or bed-clothes; quilt.

ti Also called ki, a woody plant (*Cordyline terminalis*) in the lily family, native to tropical Asia and Australia. The leaves were put to many uses by Hawaiians: for house thatch, food wrappers, hula skirt and sandals; the thick sweet roots were baked for food or distilled for brandy. Green ti leaves are still believed to afford protection from spirits and to purify a menstruating woman.

wauke Paper mulberry (*Broussonetia papyrifera*) a small tree or shrub, from eastern Asia, known throughout the Pacific for its usefulness. It belongs to the fig or mulberry family. The bark was made into tough tapa and used for clothing and bed-clothes; it lasted longer than *mamiki* tapa.

The fearsome niuhi was sometimes described as a tiger shark.

Cynthia Vanderlip

189

Bibliography

Adams, D. H. and R. H. McMichael 1999. Mercury levels in four species of sharks from the Atlantic coast of Florida. *Fishery Bulletin* 97:372-379.

Amorim, A. F., C. A. Arfelli and J. I. Castro 2000. Description of a juvenile megamouth shark, Megachasma pelagios, caught off Brazil. *Environmental Biology of Fishes* 59:117-123.

Amorim, A. F., C. A. Arfelli and L. Fagundes 1998. Pelagic elasmobranchs caught by longliners off southern Brazil during 1974-97: an overview. *Marine and Freshwater Research* 49:621-632.

Anderson, R. C. and J. D. Stevens 1996. Review of information on diurnal vertical migration in the bignose shark (Carcharhinus altimus). *Marine and Freshwater Research* 47:605-608.

Ball, P. 1999. Shark skin and other solutions. *Nature* 400:507-509.

Beckwith, M. 1970. *Hawaiian Mythology.* University of Hawai'i Press, Honolulu.

Berbari, P. and seven coauthors 1999. Antiangiogenic effects of the oral administration of liquid cartilage extract in humans. *Journal of Surgical Research* 87:108-113.

Block, B. A. and F. G. Carey 1985. Warm brain and eye temperatures in sharks. *Journal of Comparative Physiology* 156B:229-236.

Boggs, C. H. 1992. Depth, capture time, and hooked longevity of longline caught pelagic fish: timing bites of fish with chips. *Fishery Bulletin* 90:642-658.

Boggs, C. H. and R. Y. Ito 1993. Hawaii's pelagic fisheries. *Marine Fisheries Review* 55:69-82.

Boisier, P. and seven coauthors 1995. Fatal mass poisoning in Madagascar following ingestion of a shark (Carcharhinus leucas): clinical and epidemiological aspects and isolations of toxins. *Toxicon* 33:1359-1364.

Bone, Q. and A. D. Chubb 1983. The retial system of the locomotor muscles in the thresher shark. *Journal of the Marine Biological Association United Kingdom* 63:239-241.

Bonfil, R., R. Mena and D. de Anda 1993. Biological parameters of commercially exploited silky sharks, Carcharhinus falciformis, from the Campeche Bank, Mexico. pp. 73-86. In Conservation Biology of Elasmobranchs. *NOAA Technical Report* NMFS 115.

Borets, L. A. 1986 Ichthyofauna of the Northwestern and Hawaiian submarine ranges. *Journal of Ichthyology* 26:1-13.

Boustany, A.M. and five co-authors 2002. Satellite tagging: expanded niche for white sharks. *Nature* 415: 35-36.

Branstetter, S. 1987. Age, growth, and reproductive biology of the silky shark, Carcharhinus falci-formis, and the scalloped hammerhead, Sphyrna lewini, from the northwestern Gulf of Mexico. *Environmental Biology of Fishes* 19:161-174.

Bush, A. 1998. Diet, gastric evacuation, and daily ration of juvenile scalloped hammerhead sharks, Sphyrna lewini. *Pacific Science* 52:182.

Carey, F. G. and five coauthors 1982. Temperature and activities of a white shark, Carcharodon carcharias. *Copeia* :254-260.

Carey, F. G. and J. V. Scharold 1990. Movements of blue sharks (Prionace glauca) in depth and course. *Marine Biology* 106:329-342.

Casey, J. G. 1986. Distribution of the longfin mako (Isurus paucus) in the northwest Atlantic. American Society of Ichthyologists and Herpetologists/ American Elasmobranch Society annual Meeting Vitoria, British Columbia, Canada. Abstract p. 3.

Casey, J. G. and N. E. Kohler 1992. Tagging studies on the shortfin mako (Isurus oxyrinchus) in the western north Atlantic. *Australian Journal of Marine and Freshwater Research* 43:45-60.

Chave, E. H. and A. T. Jones 1991. Deep-water megafauna of the Kohala and Haleakala slopes, Alenuihaha Channel, Hawaii. *Deep Sea Research* 38:781-803.

Chave, E. H. and A. Malahoff 1998. *In Deeper Waters.* University of Hawai'i Press. Honolulu.

Chave, E. H. and B. C. Mundy 1994. Deep-sea benthic fish of the Hawaiian Archipelago, Cross Seamount, and Johnston Atoll. *Pacific Science* 48:367-409.

Chen, C. T., T. C. Leu, S. J. Joung and N. C. H. Lo 1990. Age and growth of the scalloped hammerhead, Sphyrna lewini, in northeastern Taiwan waters. *Pacific Science* 44:156-170.

Chen, C-T., K-M., Liu and Y-C. Chang 1997. Reproductive biology of the bigeye thresher shark, Alopias superciliosus (Lowe, 1839) (Chondrichthyes:Alopiidae), in the northwestern Pacific. *Ichthyological Research* 44:227-235.

Clague, D. A. and G. B. Dalrymple 1989. Tectonics, geochronology, and origin of the Hawaiian-Emperor volcanic chain. pp 188-217. *In The Geology of North America.*

Clark, E. and D.R. Nelson 1997. Young whale sharks, Rhincodon typus, feedng on a copepod bloom near La Paz, Mexico. *Environmental Biology of Fishes* 50:63-73.

Clarke, T. A. 1971. The ecology of the scalloped hammerhead shark, Sphyrna lewini, in Hawaii. *Pacific Science* 25:133-144.

Clarke, T. A. 1972. Collections and submarine observations of deep benthic fishes and decapod crustacea in Hawaii. *Pacific Science* 16:310-316.

Cobb, J. N. 1902. The commercial fisheries of the Hawaiian Islands. *Bulletin of the United States Fish Commission* 23:383-499.

Coles, R. J. 1913. Notes on the embryos of several species of rays, with remarks on the northward summer migration of certain tropical forms observed on the coast of North Carolina. *Bulletin of the American Museum of Natural History* 32:29-35.

Coles, R. J. 1916. Natural History notes on the devil fish, Manta birostris (Walbaum) and Mobula olfersi (Muller). *Bulletin of the American Museum of Natural History* 35:649-657.

Compagno, L. J. V. 1984. FAO species catalogue. Volume 4, Parts 1&2. Sharks of the World, an annotated and illustrated catalogue of shark species known to date. *FAO Fisheries Synopsis* 125:1-655.

Compagno, L. J. V. 1990. Relationships of the megamouth shark, Megachasma pelagios (Lamniformes: Megachasmidae) with comments on its feeding habits. pp. 357-379. In Elasmobranchs as living resources: advances in the biology, ecology, systematics, and the status of the fisheries. *NOAA Technical Report NMFS* 90.

Compagno, L. J. V. 1990. Shark exploitation and conservation. pp. 391-414. In Elasmobranchs as living resources: advances in the biology, ecology, systematics, and the status of the fisheries. *NOAA Technical Report NMFS* 90.

Compagno, L. J. V. 1999. Checklist of living elasmobranchs. pp. 471-498. In *Sharks, Skates, and Rays the Biology of Elasmobranch Fishes.* The Johns Hopkins University Press, Baltimore.

Compagno, L. J. V. and S. F. Cook 1996. Status of the kitefin shark Dalatias licha (Bonnaterre, 1788). *Shark News* 7:4.

Crescitelli, F. 1991. Adaptations of visual pigments to the photic environment of the deep sea. *Journal of Experimental Zoology Supplement* 5:66-75.

Crow, G. L. 1995. The reproductive biology of the tiger shark, Galeocerdo cuvier, in Hawaii: a compilation of historical and contemporary data. American Society of Ichthyologists and Herpetologists/ American Elasmobranch Society Annual Meeting Abstract p. 91.

Crow, G. L., J. Crites and R. Ito 2001. Hawaiian Islands longliner thresher shark (Alopias spp.) fishery: with comments on the absence of the common thresher shark (Alopias vulpinus) in the central north Pacific Ocean. In Preparation.

Crow, G. L. and five coauthors 1990. Protrusion of the valvular intestine through the cloaca in sharks of the family Carcharhinidae. *Copeia* :226-229.

Crow, G. L. and J. D. Hewitt IV 1988. Longevity records for captive tiger sharks Galeocerdo cuvier with notes on behaviour and management. *International Zoo Yearbook* 27:237-240.

Crow, G. L., C. G. Lowe and B. M. Wetherbee 1996. Shark records from longline fishing programs in Hawaii with comments on Pacific Ocean distributions. *Pacific Science* 80:382-392.

DeCrosta, M. A., L. R. Taylor and J. D. Parrish 1984. Age determination, growth, and energetics of three species of carcharhinid sharks in Hawaii. pp. 75-95. Proceedings of the Research Investigations of the Northwestern Hawaiian Islands UNIHI Seagrant MR-84-01.

Eckert, S. A. and B. S. Stewart 2001. Telemetry and satellite tracking of whale sharks, Rhincodon typus, in the Sea of Cortez, Mexico, and north Pacific Ocean. *Environmental Biology of Fishes* 60:299-308.

Eschmeyer, W. N. 1998. *Catalog of Fishes.* p. 483. California Academy of Sciences, San Francisco.

Fish, F. E. and L. D. Shannahan 2000. The role of the pectoral fins in body trim of sharks. *Journal of Fish Biology* 56:1062-1073.

Fowler, H. W. 1927. Fishes of the Tropical Central Pacific. *Bernice P. Bishop Museum Bulletin* 38:3-32.

Fowler, H. W. 1928. The Fishes of Oceania. *Memoirs of the Bernice P. Bishop Museum* 10:1-540.

Francis, M. P. 1996. Observations on a pregnant white shark with a review of reproductive biology. Pages 157-172. In *Great White Sharks the biology of Carcharodon carcharias.* Academic Press, New York.

Gilbert, C. H. 1905. The deep-sea fishes of the Hawaiian Islands. *Bulletin of the United States Fish Commission* 23:575-713.

Gilmore, R. G. 1983. Observations on the embryos of the longfin mako, Isurus paucus, and bigeye thresher, Alopias supercilious. *Copeia* :375-382.

Goldman, K. J. 1997. Regulation of body temperature in the white shark, Carcharodon carcharias. *Journal of Comparative Physiology* 167B:423-429.

Goldman, K. J. and Scot D. Anderson 1999. Space utilization and swimming depth of white sharks, Carcharodon carcharias, at the south Farallon Islands, central California. *Environmental Biology of Fishes* 56:351-364.

Grigg, R. W. 1988. Paleoceanography of coral reefs in the Hawaiian-Emperor chain. *Science* 240:1737-1743.

Gudger, E. W. 1914. History of the spotted eagle ray, Aetobatus narinari, together with a study of its external structures. *Papers from the Tortugas Laboratory of the Carnegie Institution of Washington* 6:241-323.

Halstead, B. W., P. S. Auerbach and D. R. Campbell 1990. *A Color Atlas of Dangerous Marine Animals.* CRC Press Inc., Florida, 192 pages.

Hamlett, W. C. (editor) 1999. Sharks, Skates, and Rays: the biology of elasmobranch fishes. Johns Hopkins University Press, Baltimore. (Many detailed chapters on anatomy and physiology).

Hoenig, J. M. and S. H. Gruber 1990. Life-history patterns in the elasmobranchs: implications for fisheries management. pp. 1-16. In Elasmobranchs as living resources: advances in the biology, ecology, systematics, and the status of the fisheries. *NOAA Technical Report* NMFS 90.

Holland, K. N., B. M. Wetherbee, C. G. Lowe and C. G. Meyer 1999. Movements of tiger sharks (Galeocerdo cuvier) in coastal Hawaiian waters. *Marine Biology* 134:665-673.

Holland, K. N., B. M. Wetherbee, J. D. Peterson, and C. G. Lowe 1993. Movements and distribution of hammerhead shark pups on their natal grounds. *Copeia* 495-502.

Holts, D. B. and D. B. Bedford 1993. Horizontal and vertical movements of the shortfin mako, Isurus oxyrinchus, in the Southern California Bight. *Australian Journal of Marine and Freshwater Research* 44:901-909.

Hubbell, G. 1996. Using tooth structure to determine the evolutionary history of the white shark. pages 9-18. In *Great White Sharks: the Biology of Carcharodon carcharias.* Academic Press, New York.

Hueter, R. E. 1991. Adaptations for spatial vision in sharks. *Journal of Experimental Zoology Supplement* 5:130-141.

Humphreys, R. L., R. B. Moffitt and M. P. Seki 1989. First record of the bigeye sand tiger shark Odontaspis noronhai from the Pacific Ocean. *Japanese Journal of Ichthyology* 36:357-362.

Humphreys, R. L., D. T. Tagami and M. P. Seki 1984. Seamount fishery resources within the southern Emperor-northern Hawaiian ridge area. Proceedings of the Resource Investigations UNIHI-Seagrant-MR-84-01 pages 283-327.

Jones, E. C. 1971. Isistius brasiliensis, a squaloid, the probable cause of crater wounds on fishes and cetaceans. *Fishery Bulletin* 69: 791-798.

Jordan, D. S. and B. W. Evermann 1905. The shore fishes of the Hawaiian Islands, with a general account of the fish fauna. *Bulletin of the United States Fish Commission* 23:1-574.

Joung, S-J., C-T Chen, E. Clark, S. Uchida and W. Y. P. Huang 1996. The whale shark, Rhincodon typus, is a livebearer: 300 embryos found in one 'mega-mamma' supreme. *Environmental Biology of Fishes* 46:219-223.

Kajiura, S. M. and T. C. Tricas 1996. Seasonal dynamics of dental sexual dimorphism in the Atlantic stingray Dasyatis sabina. *Journal of Experimental Biology* 199:2297-2306.

Kalmijn, Ad. J. 1982. Electric and magnetic field detection in elasmobranch fishes. *Science* 218:916-918.

Kamakau, S. M. 1976 *The Works of the People of Old Na Hana a ka Poe Kahiko.* Bishop Museum Press, Honolulu.

Kamakau, S. M. 1991. *Ka Poe Kahiko The people of old.* Bishop Museum Press, Honolulu.

Kane, H. K. 1996. *The 'Aumakua—Hawaiian Ancestral Spirits.* Unpublished Manuscript.

Klimley, A. P. 1993. Highly directional swimming by scalloped hammerhead sharks, Sphyrna lewini, and subsurface irradiance, temperature, bathymetry, and geomagnetic field. *Marine Biology* 117:1-22.

Klimley, A. P. and D. G. Ainley (eds) 1996. *Great White Sharks: the biology of Carcharodon carcharias.* Academic Press, San Diego 1-517 pages.

Kobayashi, H. 1986. Studies on deep-sea sharks in Kumano-nada region. *Bulletin of the Faculty of Fisheries* Mie University Number 13:25-133.

Kohler, N. 1996. NMFS cooperative shark tagging program. *Shark News* 7:1-2.

Kubota T., Y. Shiobara and T. Kubodera 1991. Food habits of the frilled shark Chlamydoselachus anguineus collected from Suruga Bay, central Japan. *Nippon Suisan Gakkaishi* 57:15-20.

Kukuyev, E. I. 1996. The new finds in recently born individuals of the whale shark Rhiniodon typus (Rhiniodontidae) in the Atlantic Ocean. *Journal of Ichthyology* 36:203-205.

Last, P. R. and J. D. Stevens 1994. *Sharks and Rays of Australia.* CSIRO, Australia.

Lavenberg, R. J. 1991. Megamania- the continuing saga of megamouth sharks. *Terra* 30:30-39.

Liu, Kwang-Ming, C-T. Chen, T-H. Liao and S-J.

Joung 1999. Age, growth. and reproduction of the pelagic thresher shark, Alopias pelagicus in the northwestern Pacific. *Copeia* :68-74.

Liu, K-M., P-J. Chiang and C-T. Chen 1997. Age and growth estimates of the bigeye thresher shark, Alopias superciliosus, in northwestern Taiwan waters. *Fishery Bulletin* 96:482-491.

Lowe, C. and G. Goodman-Lowe 1996. Suntanning in hammerhead sharks. *Nature* 383: 677.

Lowe, C. G., B. M. Wetherbee, G. L. Crow and A. L. Tester 1996. Ontogenetic dietary shifts and feeding behavior of the tiger shark, Galeocerdo cuvier, in Hawaiian waters. *Environmental Biology of Fishes* 47:203-211.

Lyle, J. M. 1984. Mercury concentrations in four carcharhinid and three hammerhead sharks from coastal waters of the northern territory. *Australian Journal of Marine and Freshwater Research* 35:441-451.

Mariano-Melendez, E. and C. Villavicencio-Garayzar 1995. Reproductive biology of the diamond stingray, Dasyatis brevis, in the western Pacific, Mexico. American Society of Ichthyologists and Herpetologists/ American Elasmobranch Society Annual Meeting Abstract page 140.

Maruska, K. P. 2001. Morphology of the mechanosensory lateral line in elasmobranch fishes: ecological and behavioral considerations. *Environmental Biology of Fishes* 60:47-75.

McCormick, H. W., T. Allen and W. E. Young 1963. *Shadows in the Sea: The sharks, skates and rays.* Weathervane Books, New York.

McCosker, J. E. 1987. The white shark, Carcharodon carcharias, has a warm stomach. *Copeia* :195-197.

McFarland, W. 1991. Light in the sea: the optical world of elasmobranchs. *Journal of Experimental Zoology Supplement* 5:3-12.

Miller, D. R., G. T. Anderson, J. J. Stark, J. L. Granick and D. Richardson 1998. Phase I/II trial of the safety and efficacy of shark cartilage in the treatment of advanced cancer. *Journal of Clinical Oncology* 16:3649-3655.

Mochizuki, K. and F. Ohe 1990. Trigonognathus kabeyai, a new genus and species of the squalid sharks from Japan. *Japanese Journal of Ichthyology* 36:385-390.

Mollet, H. F., G. Cliff, H. L. Pratt and J. D. Stevens 2000. Reproductive biology of the female short-fin mako, Isurus oxyrinchus Rafinesque 1810, with comments on the embryonic development of lamnoids. *Fishery Bulletin* 98:299-318.

Moore, K. S. and six coauthors 1993. Squalamine: an aminosterol antibiotic from the shark. *Proceedings of the National Academy of Sciences* 90:1354-1358.

Moss, S. A. 1984. *Sharks: an introduction for the amateur naturalist.* Prentice-Hall, New Jersey.

Myagkov, N. A. and V. V. Kondyurin 1976. A morphobiological description of the deepwater spiny dogfish Etmopterus lucifer (Squalidae) from west African waters. *Journal of Ichthyology* 16:1014-1018.

Myrberg, A. A. 1991. Distinctive markings of sharks: ethological considerations of visual function. *Journal of Experimental Zoology Supplement* 5:156-166.

Myrberg, A. A. 2001. The acoustical biology of elasmobranchs. *Environmental Biology of Fishes* 60:31-45.

Nakano, H., M. Okazaki and H. Okamoto 1997. Analysis of catch depth by species for tuna longline fishery based on catch by branch lines. *Bulletin of the National Research Institute Far Seas Fisheries* No. 34:43-62.

Nakano, H. and M. P. Seki 2001. Synopsis of the biological data on the blue shark, Prionace glauca Linnaeus. Manuscript in Preparation.

Nelson, D. R. and six coauthors 1997. An acoustic tracking of a megamouth shark, Megachasma pelagios: a crepuscular vertical migrator. *Environmental Biology of Fishes* 49:389-399.

Newmark, H. L. 1999. Squalene, olive oil, and cancer risk review and hypothesis. *Annals of the New York Academy of Sciences* 889:193-203.

Nishida, K. and K. Nakaya 1990. Taxonomy of the genus Dasyatis (Elasmobranchii, Dasyatiidae) from the North Pacific. pp. 327-346. In Elasmobranchs as living resources: advances in the biology, ecology, systematics, and the status of the fisheries. *NOAA Technical Report* NMFS 90.

Notarbartolo-Di-Sciara, G. 1988. Natural History of the rays of the genus Mobula in the Gulf of California. *Fishery Bulletin* 86:45-66.

Polovina, J. J. and B. B. Lau 1994. Temporal and spatial distribution of catches of tiger sharks, Galeocerdo cuvier, in the pelagic longline fishery around the Hawaiian Islands. *Marine Fisheries Review* 55:1-3.

Pooley, S. G. 1993. Hawaii's marine fisheries: some history, long-term trends, and recent developments. *Marine Fisheries Review* 55:7-19.

Pratt, H. L. jr 1979. Reproduction in the blue shark, Prionace glauca. *Fishery Bulletin* 77:445-470.

Pukui, M. K., E. W. Haertig and C. A. Lee 1972. *Nana I Ke Kumu (Look to the Source).* Volumes 1 & 2. A Queen Liliuokalani Children's Center Publication, Honolulu.

Radtke, R. L. and G. M. Cailliet 1984. Age estimation and growth of the gray reef shark Carcharhinus amblyrhynchos from the Northwestern Hawaiian Islands. pages 121-127. Proceedings of the Research Investigations of the Northwestern Hawaiian Islands. UNIHI Seagrant MR-84-01

Randall, J. E. A survey of ciguatera at Enewetok and Bikini, Marshall Islands, with notes on the systematics and food habits of ciguatoxic fishes. *Fishery Bulletin* 78:201-249.

Reeve, R. B. 1991. Hawaiian shark traditions. pages 31-38. In *Sharks Hawaii.* A. Suzumoto. Bishop Museum Press, Honolulu.

Sciarrotta, T. C. and D. R. Nelson 1977. Diel behavior of the blue shark, Prionace glauca, near Santa Catalina Island, California. *Fishery Bulletin* 75:519-528.

Seigel, J. A. and L. J. V. Compagno 1986. New records of the ragged-tooth shark, Odontaspis ferox, from California waters. *California Fish and Game* 72:172-176.

Seki, T., T. Taniuchi, H. Nakano and M. Shimizu 1998. Age, Growth and reproduction of the oceanic whitetip shark from the Pacific Ocean. *Fisheries Science* 64:14-20.

Shirai, S. and H. Tachikawa 1993. Taxonomic resolution of the Etmopterus pusillus species group (Elasmobranchii, Etmopteridae), with descriptions of E. bigelowi, n. sp. *Copeia* 483-495.

Shuttleworth, T. J. (editor) 1988. Physiology of Elasmobranch Fishes. Springer-Verlag, New York. (Many detailed chapters on anatomy and physiology).

Sills, A. K. and fifteen coauthors 1998. Squalamine inhibits angiogenesis and solid tumor growth in vivo and perturbs embryonic vasculature. *Cancer Research* 58:2784-2792.

Smith, M. M. and P. C. Heemstra 1986. *Smith's Sea Fishes*. Springer-Verlag, New York.

Smith, S. E., D. W. Au and C. Show 1998. Intrinsic rebound potentials of 26 species of Pacific sharks. *Marine and Freshwater Research* 49:663-678.

Stehmann, M. and Yu. N. Shcherbachev 1995. Second record of sixgill stingray of the genus Hexatrygon (Elasmobranchii, Hexatrygonidae) from the Indian Ocean. *Journal of Ichthyology* 35:151-159.

Stevens, J. D. (editor) 1999. *Sharks*. Checkmark, New York. (many excellent chapters).

Stevens, J. D. and K. J. McLoughlin 1991. Distribution, size and sex composition, reproductive biology and diet of sharks from northern Australia. *Australian Journal of Marine and Freshwater Research* 42:151-199.

Struhsaker, P. 1973. A contribution to the systematics and ecology of Hawaiian bathyal fishes. University of Hawai'i PhD dissertation 482 pages.

Tanaka, S. and six coauthors 1990. The reproductive biology of the frilled shark, Chamydoselachus anguineus, from Suruga Bay, Japan. *Japanese Journal of Ichthyology* 37:273-291.

Taylor, J. G. 1996. Seasonal occurrence, distibution and movement of the whale shark, Rhincodon typus, at Nigloo Reef, Wetern Australia. *Marine and Freshwater Research* 47:637-642.

Taylor, L. 1985. White Sharks in Hawaii: historical and contemporary records. *Memoirs of the Southern California Academy of Sciences* 9:41-48

Taylor, L. 1993. *Sharks of Hawaii: their biology and cultural significance.* University of Hawai'i Press, Honolulu.

Taylor, L. (editor) 1997. *The Nature Company Guides: Sharks and Rays.* Weldon Owen Group, San Francisco.

Taylor, L. R., L. J. V. Compagno and P. J. Struhsaker 1983. Megamouth—a new species, genus, and family of Lamnoid shark (Megachasma pelagios, family Megachasmidae) from the Hawaiian Islands. *Proceedings of the California Academy of Sciences* 43:87-110.

Taylor, L. and M. Wisner 1989. Growth rates of captive blacktip reef sharks (Carcharhinus melanopterus). *Bulletin de L'Institut Oceanographique*, Monaco, n0 special 5:211-217.

Titcomb, M. 1972. *Native use of fish in Hawaii.* University of Hawai'i Press, Honolulu.

Tricas, T. C. 1979. Relationships of the blue shark, Prionace glauca, and its prey species near Santa Catalina island, California. *Fishery Bulletin* 77:175-182.

Tricas, T. 1980. Courtship and mating-related behaviors in myliobatid rays. *Copeia* 553-556.

Tricas, T. C. and E. M. LeFeuvre 1985. Mating in the reef white-tip shark Triaenodon obesus. *Marine Biology* 84:233-237.

Tricas, T. C., L. R. Taylor and G. Naftel 1981. Diel behavior of the tiger shark, Galeocerdo cuvier, at French Frigate Shoals, Hawaiian Islands. *Copeia* 904-908.

Uchida, S., M. Toda and Y. Kamei 1990. Reproduction of elasmobranchs in captivity. Pages 211-237. In Elasmobranchs as Living Resources: Advances in the Biology, Ecology, Systematics and the Status of Fisheries. *NOAA Technical Report* 90.

Uchida, S., M. Toda, K. Teshima, K, Yano 1996. Pregnant white sharks and full-term embryos from Japan. Pages 139-155. In *Great white sharks: the biology of Carcharodon carcharias.* Academic Press, New York.

Walker, G. P. L. 1990. Geology and volcanology of the Hawaiian Islands. *Pacific Science* 44:315-347.

About the Authors

GERALD L. CROW, Research Associate III at the University of Hawai'i's Waikīkī Aquarium, has been a noted scientific researcher in the field of marine biology for 20 years and has published twenty refereed research papers—many of them on sharks—in journals such as *Zoo Biology, Journal of Parasitology, Journal of Experimental Zoology, Pacific Science, Coral Reefs, Journal of Wildlife Diseases,* and *Environmental Biology of Fishes.* In addition, he has authored articles for a number of popular publications, and is a sought-after speaker at community seminars and marine biology conferences worldwide—including the prestigious Monterey Bay Aquarium Research Institute, International Association of Aquatic Animal Medicine, and the Hawai'i Institute of Marine Biology at Coconut Island.

His research has centered on the ecology of coastal and pelagic sharks, the evaluation of shark-control programs, and shark physiology. Other studies have targeted individual species such as the tiger, Galapagos, gray reef and sixgill sharks.

He has appeared on several television programs including *Tales of the Tiger Shark,* aired during the Discovery Channel's Shark Week; is regularly interviewed by radio, newspaper and other media; has been quoted extensively in the Discovery Channel's book, *Sharks! The Mysterious Killers;* and serves on the Hawai'i Shark Task Force. He is an active member of several professional groups including the Wildlife Disease Association, International Association for Aquatic Animal Medicine, American Zoological Association and American Elasmobranch Society, for which he has recently completed a two-year stint on the Board of Directors' Executive Committee.

He heads the shark research program at the Waikīkī Aquarium, and his latest shark-related projects include research into the causes of thyroid hyperplasia (goiter) in sharks, the tiger shark reproductive system, and the distribution of thresher sharks in Hawaiian waters. During the summer, he also teaches week-long shark-biology classes—through the University of Hawai'i at Hilo and the Oceanic Society—at Midway Atoll in the Northwestern Hawaiian Islands. And he is currently conducting a multiyear shark-tagging research project, also at Midway.

JENNIFER CRITES is a freelance writer, editor and photographer who has written about Hawaiian culture, travel, business, environmental issues, parenting and other subjects for a variety of publications including *Islands, Honolulu Magazine, The Rotarian, The Hollywood Reporter, Location Update,* HMSA's *Island Scene, Hawaiian Airlines Magazine, Hawaii Parent,* UH's *Malamalama,* and *Fodor's Hawai'i '98* and *'99* travel guides. During her tenure as managing editor of Davick Publications' *ALOHA, the Magazine of Hawai'i and the Pacific,* she helped produce *Islands of Aloha,* the Hawai'i Visitors and Convention Bureau's guide to Hawai'i. And she is an editorial consultant for several businesses.

For three years, Jennifer volunteered as a docent in the Waikīkī Aquarium's School Support Program, where she taught children in grades kindergarten through six about life in the ocean. Currently, her column—Hawai'i's Sharks—is featured in the Around Town section of Road Runner Hawai'i's online community website, www.hawaii.rr.com.

In addition to writing nature articles for children's magazines, including a story on "Shark Sense" for the award-winning national publication W.O.W. *(Wild Outdoor World),* Jennifer loves to snorkel and has explored undersea coral reefs off the coasts of California, Hawai'i and the islands of Micronesia.